Signposts

Derek Tidball

Signposts

A devotional map
of the Psalms

ivp

INTER-VARSITY PRESS
Norton Street, Nottingham NG7 3HR, England
Email: ivp@ivpbooks.com
Website: www.ivpbooks.com

First published 2009
Reprinted 2010

British Library Cataloguing in Publication Data
A catalogue record for this book is available from the British Library.

ISBN: 978-1-84474-373-5

Set in Dante 11/14pt
Typeset in Great Britain by CRB Associates, Potterhanworth, Lincolnshire
Printed in Great Britain by Ashford Colour Press Ltd, Gosport, Hampshire

Inter-Varsity Press publishes Christian books that are true to the Bible and that communicate the gospel, develop discipleship and strengthen the church for its mission in the world.

Inter-Varsity Press is closely linked with the Universities and Colleges Christian Fellowship, a student movement connecting Christian Unions in universities and colleges throughout Great Britain, and a member movement of the International Fellowship of Evangelical Students. Website: *www.uccf.org.uk*

Dedicated to
Jenny, Peter and Nick Aston,
with thanks for true friendship

Contents

Introduction

Psalm

1	The great divide
2	The laughing God
3	Falling apart
4	Seeking God's smile
5	Listen to my cry
	Meditating on God's law
6	When all you have is tears
7	Justice for the innocent
8	The crown of creation
9	The Lord is known for his justice
10	The wicked exposed
	The justice of God
11	When stability is threatened
12	Economical with the truth
13	How long, O Lord?
14	When fools speak
15	Who is acceptable?
	'The Maker of heaven and earth'
16	Fullness of joy
17	The apple of your eye
18	God floodlights my life
19	Words, words and more words
20	Victory in the name of the Lord
	The God who saves me
21	Rejoicing in God's strength
22	My God, my God, why?
23	The Good Shepherd
24	The arrival of the King
25	The friendship of the Lord
	Covenant love

26   Declare me innocent

27   The Lord is my light

28   The Lord is . . .

29   The voice of the Lord

30   But rejoicing comes in the morning

God's activity in history

31   My life in God's hands

32   The hiding place

33   Sing joyfully because . . .

34   Tasting the Lord's goodness

35   Thanks through the tears

The Lord reigns

36   Wicked men and loving God

37   Cool down

38   Crushing blows

39   Just a-passing through

40   True to experience

Zion and the temple

41   Blessed are the merciful

42   Spiritual depression

43   Send me your light

44   Why are you hiding, Lord?

45   A wedding song for the king

Exile and return

46   Be still and know

47   Ascension

48   Breathtaking Jerusalem

49   'Death after life does greatly please'

50   Summoning the earth

'The name of the Lord is to be praised'

51   Whatever happened to sin?

52   So much for heroes!

53   Those fools again

54   The name of the Lord

55   When friends fail

Give thanks to the Lord

56   When fear strikes
57   Beneath the shadow of his wings
58   Break their teeth
59   Surrounded by snarling dogs
60   A prayer for desperate times
      Affirmations of faith
61   The rock that is higher
62   Finding rest in God
63   A God for everywhere
64   A battle of arrows
65   Intimacy and awe
      'Trust in the Lord'
66   How awesome are your deeds
67   May God be gracious to us
68   Majesty and meekness
69   I am in trouble
70   Seekers
      'I'm hurting': Personal lament
71   Faithful to the end
72   And he shall reign
73   It's not fair, God
74   O God, defend your cause
75   God is near
      'We're hurting': Community lament
76   The boldest claim
77   Fond memories of songs in the night
78   When will they ever learn?
79   God of our salvation
80   Turn us
      'Blot out my transgressions'
81   The seasons of worship
82   The judge of judges
83   Don't sit idly by, Lord
84   My soul yearns
85   The perfect balance
      'Curse them, Lord': Psalms of vengeance

86	Is it OK to ask this?
87	Glorious things are said of you
88	Waiting in the dark
89	Former love?
90	Lord of the generations

'Teach me your ways, Lord': Wisdom psalms

91	The shelter of the most high
92	'Nothing but goodness'
93	The Lord reigns
94	The avenging God
95	Let us worship

A quick reference guide

96	Among the nations
97	Let the earth be glad
98	Sing and shout
99	Exalt the Lord
100	Jubilate

The beauty of the Psalms: Poetry

101	A life of integrity
102	My days . . . your years
103	Forget not all his benefits
104	Clothed with splendour
105	Remember the wonders

Five books or one?

106	The tragedy of spiritual amnesia
107	Let the redeemed give thanks
108	Immovable
109	Is anger OK?
110	The Priest-King

Who wrote the Psalms?

111	Hallelujah!
112	People who are blessed
113	From height to depth
114	Exodus and the earth
115	Not to us, Lord

'Make music to the Lord'

116	Precious to God
117	The shortest psalm
118	Love actually
119	Revelling in God's law
120	On being a nonconformist

The Psalms and festivals

121	Help from the Lord
122	Pray for Jerusalem
123	Till he shows mercy
124	But for the Lord
125	Always God's people

The Psalms and the Messiah

126	We dreamed
127	Unless the Lord
128	Fear and fruitfulness
129	Persecution and perseverance
130	Plenteous redemption

The Psalms and the life of Jesus

131	Contentment
132	The swearing of oaths
133	A hint of heaven
134	The nightwatchmen
135	He does whatever he pleases

The Psalms and the cross of Jesus

136	His faithfulness endures
137	Weeping
138	Dimensions of praise
139	O God, you know
140	You are my God

The Psalms and the apostle Paul

141	A serious spirituality
142	No-one cares
143	Give me a firm footing
144	Divine strength, human weakness
145	A symphony of praise

The Psalms and the letter to the Hebrews P. 191

146   Why God is worth trusting

147   How right it is to praise God

148   Heaven and earth

149   A new song

150   A fitting crescendo

             The Psalms and the book of Revelation

Afterword

For reference and further reading

Introduction

This book grew out of a period of intense need in my life. For years it has been my practice to begin my daily devotions with the reading of a psalm. It would be untrue to claim that they have always spoken appositely to my situation, but it is amazing how often they have and how useful they have proved during the day in encouraging others. But then, at a time of particular difficulty, they became my vital source of hope, as they directed me to God, his rebuke and his discipline, but also to his unfailing love and forgiveness. They have been anything but mere words to me. With the help of the Holy Spirit they have connected me again to the one who proves unerringly to be our rock, our refuge, our shield, our strength, our stronghold, our sun, our deliverer, our guide, our sufficiency, our Sovereign and our King. They show an acute awareness that our lives lie in his hands.

The Psalms have, of course, been the oxygen of corporate worship and private devotion for God's people for generations. Since they were composed they have had an extraordinary ability to enable people to give voice to joy, praise and thanksgiving, and an equal ability to turn their fears, frustrations, anxieties and failures into heartfelt prayer to God. The whole of life is to be found in them, the complete range of emotions and the raw reality of our precarious existence. They speak to and for everyone, whatever their situation, and suck everyone in, no matter what the state of their heart.

Having said that, the Psalms can be a very confusing book, not least because of its length and seeming lack of organization. I can understand why some find the psalms repetitive and hard to digest except by chewing on a morsel here and there. Poetry can be hard to navigate and one bit can easily blur into another. This book is an attempt to help such people. Imagine it as providing a map. Maps are designed to help you find your way, watch out for points of interest and make connections between one place and another. This is what I have aimed to do for each psalm. A brief introduction provides an *Orientation*, a *Map* helps to chart one's way through the psalm, and this is very occasionally followed by *Links* which make connections with elsewhere. A final section, *Signpost*, points away from the psalm and directs the reader to a point of action, a way of responding, or a key theme that is developed elsewhere. I have felt free not to follow this formula rigidly. Where appropriate, the names mentioned in the *Signposts* have been changed.

Looking at a signpost, it should be said, is no substitute for travelling the road and experiencing the destination for yourself. Usually a map is mere preparation for the real adventure and a signpost an anticipation of what is to come. This book will be valuable only if you have your Bible open alongside it and experience the psalm, and the God of whom it speaks, for yourself. More often than not, maps require careful study. A casual glance is not only insufficient, but may prove positively misleading. So, the Psalms require a little time if they are to prove beneficial: a rushed reading of them is likely to yield little and may even end up being frustratingly unhelpful.

Signposts are designed for specific purposes, some to point to a distant town, some to point out a tourist attraction and some to give information about the road itself. They even look different, with those on motorways, A and B roads and others all having their own shape, colour and layout. So here, while the 'sign' for each psalm follows a similar pattern, after every fifth psalm another kind of sign has been included. These short articles are designed to give a quick overview of a theme or topic that concerns the Psalms as a whole, or at least a significant number of them.

No signpost can draw attention to everything. So here an awful lot is missed out, particularly concerning scholarly discussion, which could profitably be included. But that can be found in the numerous good commentaries on the Psalms. At the end I have listed those from which I have quoted. I did not want to clutter the pages with footnotes, but the source of the quotations should be easily identifiable. I am sure I have unconsciously repeated phrases, ideas or material I have picked up from others over the years but have now lost track of the source. I apologize if there is unintentionally insufficient acknowledgment.

The exercise of writing these notes grew from my need at a testing period in my life to make more sense of the Psalms that I had been reading for years. I do not claim the approach will suit everyone, but if some who read this can chart their way through the Psalms better and find their way to the God for all seasons as a result, it will have served its purpose. I also hope it will unlock the Psalms in a way that proves useful to those who are called to preach on them.

As always, my thanks are due to many others who have helped in the publication of this book. I am grateful yet again for the perceptive comments of Alec Motyer, who helpfully pointed out ways of improving what I had written, and of Kate Byrom and the team at IVP, who creatively developed an unusual manuscript. The book is dedicated to Jenny, Peter and Nick Aston in thankfulness for their wonderful friendship.

Derek Tidball

Psalm 1

 ORIENTATION: Psalm 1 serves as a suitable introduction to the whole of the Psalms because of its uncomplicated delight in God's law. The Psalms, like the writings associated with Moses, are arranged in five books and share an emphasis on the importance of God's law, the essence of which lies, not in legal stipulations, but in an understanding of his ways. Psalm 1 divides the world sharply into two groups – the godly and the godless. The godly know God's blessing; the wicked experience his judgment.

MAP: This psalm is the most basic of all and introduces:

The godly, 1–3

In introducing the godly, the Psalmist gives us:

- a warning to note, 1. His thought shows a progression, warning against increasing involvement with the ungodly, from walking (casual acquaintance) to standing (lingering) and finally sitting (belonging).
- a pattern to follow, 2. Godliness grows from paying careful and joyful attention to God's word.
- an ambition to have, 3. To be an evergreen and fruitful tree in dry and dusty Israel was something to be prized.

The godless, 4–5

Note the strong contrast between the godly and the godless – 'not so the wicked':

- their existence is empty, 4b: 'chaff';
- their life is precarious, 4c: 'blows away';
- their destiny is destruction, 5.

LINKS: Verse 6 provides a succinct summary of the psalm. Deut. 30:15–20 and Matt. 7:13–14, 24–27 dwell on the same theme.

SIGNPOST: Some of the trees in our garden are flourishing, but others are diseased and need treatment while one evergreen recently died from lack of water and had to be removed. Which sort of tree characterizes my life with God? How much do I love God's law and build my life and relationships around it? Am I tempted to linger around those who are unhelpful to my being a follower of Jesus and am I being drawn away from him?

Psalm 2

ORIENTATION: This shocking psalm offends modern sensibilities as God laughs not in humour, but in derision at the nations. The nations are an example of 'the wicked' spoken about in Psalm 1. Many view it as a second introduction because the theme of kingship is prominent in the Psalms.

MAP: This map is drawn on a cosmic scale and features:

The rebellion of the nations, 1–3

They are characterized by engaging in:

- frenetic activity, 1, in plotting and conspiring;
- futile alliances, 2, in banding together;
- foolish ambitions, 3, in seeking independence from God.

The derision of the Lord, 4–6

- God's reaction is to laugh at their folly, 4.
- God's response is to rebuke their wilfulness, 5.
- God's rebuttal is to re-establish his authority, 6, by installing his own king on the throne.

The dominion of the son, 7–9

The king is God's son and these verses speak of his:

- unique relationship to the Father, 7;
- universal rule over the earth, 8;
- uncompromising judgment on his enemies, 9.

The reflection of the onlooker, 10–12

Reflecting on this, a commentator invites the nations to:

- choose wisdom and take warning, 10;
- serve reverently, 11;
- submit humbly to the son's rule, 12.

LINKS: The early Christians saw it as speaking of Jesus' kingly rule: Matt. 3:17; Acts 4:25–26; 13:32–33; Heb. 1:5–6; Rev. 2:7; 12:5; 19:15.

SIGNPOST: Tony Blair's spokesman famously said that as UK prime minister Blair didn't 'do God'. But can politicians avoid 'doing God'? And isn't it good that they hold themselves accountable to the supreme authority in the universe? This psalm assumes a big God who is more powerful than the superpowers who conspire against him. Is my God this big? Do I really believe he holds nations accountable? If so, how does that fuel my attitudes and prayers?

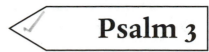

ORIENTATION: Set in the time of his son Absalom's rebellion (2 Sam. 15 – 17), this psalm reflects one of the lowest points of David's reign when he was threatened with losing everything he had accomplished. Life was falling apart.

MAP: Here are the contours of faith.

The valley: the enemies he faced, 1–2

David expresses what he feels about his enemies:

- their numbers, 1: 'many'. Kidner speaks of 'a rising tide of disloyalty';
- their character, 2: accusing, cynical, faithless;
- their falsehood, 2: in saying God has deserted David.

The mountaintop: the God he trusted, 3–7

Note the active verbs. God 'lifts my head high', 'answers me', 'sustains me'. In dire circumstances, God is:

- a protective shield, 3;
- a ready listener, 4;
- a sustaining presence, 5–6;
- an active saviour, 7.

The plateau: the faith he expressed, 8

When faced with trouble we often look to people for support, but David expresses his confidence in God as the one who will deliver him.

LINKS: Although the psalm arises out of an extreme situation, verses 5–6 make it 'also an evening psalm for the ordinary believer' (Kidner), helping them to view their everyday troubles in the context of faith. 1 Pet. 5:7 may aptly be said to summarize the psalm: 'Cast all your anxiety on him because he cares for you.'

SIGNPOST: An inability to sleep is one of the warning signs of stress, depression or, ironically, exhaustion. It is often accompanied by anxiety or a foolish desire to control what we cannot control. Yet here is David in the most extreme of situations sleeping well because of his faith in God. Do I believe that my God is the God of David? If so, can I leave my situations of extreme difficulty and my everyday troubles in his hands? Do I turn to God as a first or a last resort? And how does this active trust in God differ from complacency or an avoidance of responsibility?

Seeking God's smile

 ORIENTATION: The prayer, 'Let the smile of your face shine on us, Lord' (NLT, v. 6), is the climax of the psalm which functions as a primer on prayer.

MAP: This elementary guide to prayer highlights:

The heart of prayer, 1

- The cry for help. 'Mercy' here is not a quest for forgiveness for wrongdoing, since David believes himself to be sinned against rather than a sinner (2–3), but for relief from distress. David has come to the end of his own resources and believes only God can help.

The occasion of prayer, 2

- A situation of need and distress caused by enemies, who 'long for nothing but trash and lies' (Jackson). We know nothing of the specific circumstances except that people have sought to humiliate David and question his honour and dignity.

The certainty of prayer, 3

- The Lord will answer, because the one who prays is a 'faithful servant'.

The attitude of prayer, 4–5

- Right attitudes are essential. We cannot come to God harbouring sin or with anger that has been permitted to fester. These verses are taken up in Matt. 5:23–26 and Eph. 4:26.

The fruit of prayer, 6–8

Here is a wonderful picture of a relationship with God that in the setting is anything but complacent. It speaks of:

- the smile of God, 6;
- sufficiency from God, 7;
- security in God, 8.

SIGNPOST: Charles Spurgeon said of his friend, the evangelist J. Manton Smith, that seeing his smile was as good as taking a fortnight's holiday. Whether a person smiles, frowns or feigns indifference makes all the difference in the world in a relationship. How would I characterize my relationship with God? Do I feel his smile, or am I experiencing his frown? Worse still, am I finding it difficult to see him at all? If I am enjoying his smile, am I letting it permeate every part of my life and am I therefore able to be secure even in the face of my enemies? If I am not enjoying his smile, why not? How can his smile be recovered?

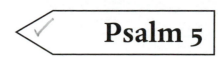

ORIENTATION: This is an urgent individual lament in which anguish is expressed throughout. 'The reality of life on earth frustrates the full joy of the godly. Fears swell up in our hearts as we contemplate the harshness of life' (VanGemeren). When that happens, the only solace is to be found in prayer.

MAP: Like Psalm 4, this psalm gives us another basic pattern for prayer.

The basis of our prayer, 1–7

We can be confident in our praying because of the one to whom we pray. David's prayer is founded on:

- the sovereignty of God, 2: 'my King';
- the covenant of God, 2, 7: 'my God'. God and David are personally committed to each other (see note on 'Covenant love', p. 46);
- the holiness of God, 4–6: 'you are not a God who is pleased with wickedness'.

The manner of our prayer, 3, 7

It should be a matter of:

- priority, 3: 'in the morning';
- patience, 3: 'wait expectantly';
- confidence, 7: 'come into your house';
- humility, 7: 'in reverence'.

The content of our prayer, 8–12

- direction for God's servants, 8;
- judgment on God's enemies, 9–10: 'for they have rebelled against you';
- protection for God's friends, 11–12.

The psalm ends on a note of trustful affirmation, having set out the why (1–7), how (3, 7) and what (8–12) of prayer when facing trouble.

SIGNPOST: On one occasion, well-meaning church members accused me publicly of failing in my leadership because I did not take the whole church down the particular path they had travelled with the Holy Spirit. They were good friends and it hurt. But this conflict was resolved when I prayed about it (as with other similarly painful situations). The connection is not coincidental! So why am I so reluctant to 'take it to the Lord in prayer', as the hymn 'What A Friend We Have In Jesus' puts it? Can I use this psalm as a model for my daily prayer life?

Meditating on God's law

The encouragement to meditate on God's law frequently occurs in the Bible, not just in the Psalms. Joshua, for example, is told, 'Keep this Book of the Law always on your lips; meditate on it day and night, so that you may be careful to do everything written in it' (Josh. 1:8). Future kings were instructed to write it out, read it and apply it daily so they would learn to revere God (Deut. 17:18–19). The law reveals the mind of God and teaches the ways of God. Knowing his law is the secret to knowing him.

God's law is presented in various styles and found in numerous places. It refers, for example, not only to the collection of commandments such as those found in the opening five books of the Bible, but to the instructions given by a father to his son in Proverbs.

Psalms 1, 19 and 119 make this law their major theme while others, such as 18, 25, 78, 89, 105, 147 and 148, refer to it. Its importance lies not only in that it is a revelation of God's heart, but also in that to live in harmony with it brings blessing and prosperity, while to live in conflict with it, or in indifference to it, brings the reverse.

Meditation on Scripture takes time, a commodity most of us seem to be short of today. Yet ironically, many non-Christians have adopted other forms of meditation as a way of searching for peace and wholeness in their busy lives. Biblical meditation has a long tradition and is a secret many of us need to rediscover and reclaim. It is a way of ensuring that the law becomes a part of us, so that we might, as it were, after a time almost live by it instinctively.

To meditate is to chew over, to ponder, to ruminate, to digest some particular aspect of God's word, in his presence, with a receptive not an argumentative heart, and to apply it to one's life. Don't run before you can walk. Choose a quiet place and time, and begin with perhaps just five minutes going over prayerfully in your mind a verse from the Psalms that has spoken to you.

ORIENTATION: Classed as the first of seven penitential psalms, it is not clear whether its background is sickness and healing, or guilt and forgiveness. Sinfulness is clearly the background to the psalm, but no specific sin is mentioned. We cannot tell the circumstances of the psalm, though Absalom's rebellion (see Ps. 3) is possible. It abruptly changes direction in v. 8, where there is 'finally an outburst of defiant faith' (Kidner).

 MAP: These are the steps David takes here:

He requests, 1–2
He asks for mercy in the sense of:
- an avoidance of God's anger, 1;
- a healing of the body's sickness, 2.

He reasons, 3–5
Mercy is requested in view of:
- the length of his suffering, 3: 'How long?'
- the faithfulness of God's love, 4b;
- the futility of death's domain, (until Christ).

He recounts, 6–7
His suffering is characterized by:
- weariness;
- weeping;
- weakness.

He revives, 8–10
Prayer revives his spirit and gives him renewed confidence:
- to confront his enemies, 8, 10;
- to trust his God, 9.

LINKS: The other penitential psalms are 32, 38, 51, 102, 130 and 143.

SIGNPOST: Kidner suggests this prayer provides words for 'those who scarcely have the heart to pray, and brings them within sight of victory'. It is sometimes difficult to pray for a whole host of reasons. Many years ago, after a bout of illness, I hardly had the energy to pray and praying a psalm a day was all I could manage. But how it lifts the spirit! Aren't there times when we are so at the end of our own resources that downloading our failings and pressures on God is all we can do? And doesn't this bring 'sweet relief'?

Psalm 7

ORIENTATION: *Shiggaion* is an unknown musical term, used only here in the Psalms (and in Hab. 3:1), possibly associated with strong, turbulent emotions. This is essentially the cry of an innocent person for justice, but it is more than a lament and contains notes that celebrate God's kingship. Life is often not straightforward and can stir up a jumble of conflicting emotions. Here, anger and anguish jostle with confession and confidence, tragedy with trust and triumph.

 MAP: The psalm unfolds as:

Petition is made to God, 1–2

David prays for protection and deliverance from his vicious enemies. We know nothing of Cush, mentioned in the title, but the tribe of Benjamin harboured a number of David's enemies (2 Sam. 16:11; 19:16–23).

Innocence is protested before God, 3–4

He throws himself on God, trusting that the Lord will see he is not to blame for provoking the conflict.

Justice is sought from God, 5–9

He approaches God as the judge, who presides in his heavenly court and dispenses perfect justice on behalf of the wronged. He wants God to 'close the book on evil' (*The Message*).

Testimony is given about God, 10–13

The plea for justice gives way to an affirmation of God as 'a righteous judge'.

Judgment is exercised by God, 14–16

God exercises judgment, often by evil rebounding on its perpetrators.

Confidence is expressed in God, 17

The psalmist does not take God's justice for granted, but joyfully expresses thanks for it.

SIGNPOST: Recent years have seen the dramatic downfall of many tyrants. While historians explain events in secular terms, many have commented on the spiritual factors involved. Erich Honecker's East German regime fell after prayer meetings in Leipzig attracted thousands of intercessors. Pastors were key to the Romanian Revolution. When Ceausescu fell, 150,000 thousand knelt before Timisoara's cathedral, prayed the Lord's Prayer and chanted, 'God exists. There is a God.' Evidence of God's justice at work today setting oppressed people free is abundant. Do you believe in such a God, the God of Psalm 7?

 ORIENTATION: Psalm 8, like a number of others, is structured as a chiasmus. A chiasmus is an X-shaped structure where the first part crosses over with the second part, or the first part finds itself reversed in the second (see Ps. 9 for a further example). Here we have benediction (vv. 1, 9), God's rule *v.* human rule (vv. 2–3, 6–8), human insignificance *v.* human significance (vv. 4, 5). While this psalm begins and ends with the majesty of God filling the earth, the substance concerns humans as 'the crown of creation' (Kidner).

MAP: The psalm speaks of:

God and human instinct, 2
Children sense their relationship with God and instinctively praise him, even if religious sophisticates (Matt. 21:16) and arrogant intellectuals do not.

God and human dignity, 3–5
The puny nature of human beings is contrasted with the immensity of the cosmos. Paradoxically, this magnifies the dignity of human beings who are 'crowned with glory' since God saw them and designed them as (literally) 'little gods'. This doesn't imply divinity, but under God humans have an exalted status in creation. This looks like an early, and godly, version of the anthropic principle of which scientists speak, which claims that human beings are the real centre and point of the creation. See Gen. 1:27.

God and human responsibility, 6–8
The status leads to responsibility to care for creation, as set out in Gen. 1:28–30.

LINKS: Heb. 2:6–10 reflects on these words and finds them ultimately fulfilled in the one perfect human there ever was, Jesus.

SIGNPOST: This is a true story. A rich friend of mine went to a garage to buy a Rolls-Royce, but the salesman clumsily used the wrong sales tactic. 'Buy this car, Mr Jones,' he said, 'and it will give you real status.' 'Nonsense,' replied my friend, 'I'm a human being. This is a lump of metal. I am the one who will lend the car status.' He never bought the Rolls and drove a battered old Volvo instead! He had good theology, if not good taste. Do we sometimes give a higher value to things than to people, the summit of God's creation?

Psalm 9

The Lord is known for his justice

ORIENTATION: This positive psalm expresses thanks for and pays tribute to God's justice (v. 16). It is an incomplete acrostic. In acrostics the first letter of each line starts with a different letter of the alphabet in order. They reflect the 'orderliness and symmetry of the poem's contents' (Brueggemann). Many see the first part as the voice of an individual (vv. 1–10) and the second as the voice of the community (vv. 11–20), but it is also structured as a chiasmus (see Ps. 8).

 MAP: Its elegant structure is as follows:

A *1–2, Prayer of gratitude:* 'I will praise you, Lord.'

 B *3–4, Present justice leads to enemy defeat:* God is actively at work in providing justice in the present.

 C *5–6, The nations: the principle of justice stated:* The psalmist's personal experience of justice is transformed into a more general, international principle.

 D *7–8, God is sovereign:* reigning over his world and its peoples.

 E *9–10, Expression of trust:* Far from being an impersonal and removed ruler, God can be trusted, especially by the victims and the vulnerable in society.

 E¹ *11–12, Expression of praise:* Trust is turned into praise.

 D¹ *13–14, God is saviour:* The psalmist moves from affirming God's power to praying that God will use it to deliver him.

 C¹ *15–16, The nations: the practice of justice stated:* Again, the psalmist moves from stating the principle of God's justice to a celebration of its practice.

 B¹ *17–18, Future justice ensures complete enemy defeat:* He is confident that what God has begun in the present (3–4) he will complete in the future.

A¹ *19–20, Prayer of petition:* 'Arise, Lord.'

SIGNPOST: Do I have enemies? As a Christian I am not supposed to have any, and, if I have, I am supposed to love them. The psalmist is less inhibited. His enemies, however, are not people he simply dislikes, but those who are defying God's law. Can I be honest with myself about the enemies I have? Are they people who have really done wrong, or merely those to whom I've taken a personal dislike? Do I share the psalmist's concern for God's honour? Am I content to leave justice in his hands? How often have I found v. 9 to be true?

ORIENTATION: Psalm 10 completes the acrostic begun in Psalm 9. In the context of forceful prayer (v. 1) and an acknowledgment of God using his kingship on behalf of victims (vv. 16–18), the psalm spends most time providing an anatomy of the wicked. Wilcock says that Psalm 9 is positive and 10 negative. They picture the same circumstances, but 'one is bright with dark shadows, the other dark with bright gleams'.

MAP: The wicked, as the psalmist feels strongly, are:

Cunning, 2: 'the schemes they devise';
Greedy, 3: 'the cravings of their hearts';
Godless, 4: 'there is no room for God';
Arrogant, 5–6: 'they sneer . . . "Nothing will ever shake us"';
Dishonest, 7: 'full of lies';
Violent, 8–10: 'they lie in wait . . . ' (×3) ' . . . to catch the helpless';
Presumptuous, 11, 13: 'God . . . never sees . . . He won't call us to account.'

Having pointed out this ignorance of God, the psalm begins to focus on God, even if in something of an angry way. God is watching and this is aimed not at harming the helpless, but at defending them (v. 12). He sees 'the trouble of the afflicted' (v. 14).

SIGNPOST: 'Where is God when you need him? Why is life so difficult?' cried a friend who limped through life from one crisis to another. He faced redundancy, poor health, vandalism and family pressures in short order. He was perplexed as to why God stood 'far off' (v. 1) while others, who were spiritually indifferent, breezed through life with ease. He kept afloat because underneath it all he believed that the unseen God knew 'the hopes of the helpless' (v. 17, NLT) and was listening to his cry. Larry Crabb wrote that even 'healthy people experience a marred joy. For them, life is lived in the minor key, but with an eager anticipation of the day when the Master Musician will strike up the eternal anthem in the major key'. They know all is not right and 'long for a better day, confident that it will come, but groaning until it does' (*Understanding People*, Marshall Pickering, 1987). If that's true of healthy people, think what music will strike up when my friend, and others like him, arrive at 'the better day'!

The justice of God

A major theme of the Psalms is a belief in God's justice. Wrung from their experience of injustice, time and again, the psalmists cry out for God to come to their defence and execute justice on their behalf.

The cry for justice is not founded on a belief in some impersonal force, but on the character of God. It isn't that 'all will work out in the end', but that God will vindicate the wronged and judge the wrongdoers. He 'loves justice' (11:7; 99:4) because he is righteous and morally uncorrupted (7:9; 11:7; 77:13; 85:13; 89:18; 119:137). He is able to execute justice because he reigns as sovereign over his world (9:7–8; 22:28). His commitment to justice means he has a special concern for those who are unable to speak up for themselves because of their poverty, lowly status or vulnerable position in society (10:17–18; 68:5–6; 82:3–4). The psalmists were basing their prayers on the revelation of God given in Deut. 10:17–21, which was at the heart of Israel's faith.

Crying for justice testifies to a faith that grapples with living in the real world. It does not live in a fantasy world in which all is sweetness and light, as contemporary worship sometimes pretends. It recognizes that wickedness is both real and powerful, and equally that strong emotions and reactions are pent up inside most of us when we encounter it.

Crying for justice from God is a wise way of dealing with evil. It dumps the problem in God's lap and so helps us to avoid either repressing negative emotions, which is unhealthy, or taking the law into our own hands, which leads us to retaliation and vengeance. Our hope of ultimate justice lies with God alone. Leaving God to sort out injustice is what lies behind Jesus' teaching on non-retaliation and is why Christians can love their enemies (Matt. 5:38–48). Paul wrote, 'Do not take revenge, my dear friends, but leave room for God's wrath, for it is written: "It is mine to avenge; I will repay," says the Lord' (Rom. 12:19).

ORIENTATION: Life, as David has known it, is falling apart (v. 3). All its familiar certainties are collapsing. Probably reflecting the time when Saul is hunting him like a deer, David's faith is severely tested (see 1 Sam. 26:17–20), even if it comes through triumphant in the end.

MAP: The psalmist journeys through less-charted territory where:

Faith is shaken, 1–3

Because of:

- the advice of his friends, 1. Their well-meaning but misdirected advice has encouraged his escapism.
- the attack of his enemies, 2.
- the assault on his foundations, 3. His assumptions about morality and order are thrown into confusion.

Faith is sustained, 4–7

Faith holds on in spite of the above because he has a firm understanding of God. Verse 4 begins a strong counter-offensive to the attack on his faith.

- God's presence is secure, 4a: he is 'in his holy temple'.
- God's rule is ongoing, 4b: he is 'on his heavenly throne'.
- God's vision is unimpaired, 4c: 'he observes'.
- God's standards are unaltered, 5: he still hates the wicked.
- God's judgment is certain, 6: 'he will . . .'
- God's love is trustworthy, 7: 'the upright will see his face'.

SIGNPOST: Escapism may have a place in helping us to enjoy a healthy lifestyle, but when David's friends tell him (v. 1) that the answer to his problems lies in escapism, they're wrong. It is impossible to avoid some problems. They need to be faced rather than avoided. And with God's help they can be overcome. Some escapism is good and healthily recreative. What are my favourite forms of escapism – the soaps, sport, reading novels, holidays? Are these wholesome recreations that help me face the challenges of life and rebuild my faith, or do they unwisely assist me in ignoring problems and shirking responsibilities? How much time do they take up? When I face severe problems, do I have faith in the God whom David trusts, or do I seek an escape route?

When stability is threatened

ORIENTATION: At the heart of this psalm lies the contrast between what 'they' say (v. 4) and what the Lord replies (v. 5).

MAP: Three different voices are heard in the psalm.

The foolish voice of the people, 1–4

The psalmist claims that 'everyone' (a generalization) speaks:

- empty words, 2a: 'lies' that are insincere;
- manipulative words, 2b–3a: 'flatter with their lips';
- deceitful words, 2c: 'harbour deception in their hearts';
- arrogant words, 3b–4: 'boastful tongue'.

They speak like this because they are godless (1, 4).

The wise voice of the Lord, 5–6

In contrast, God's words are:

- concerned for the poor, not the powerful, 5;
- effective because they're active, not empty, 5b;
- trustworthy because they're proven, not untested, 6.

The plaintive voice of the needy, 1, 7–8

The third voice is that of the psalmist himself, speaking on behalf of the needy:

- their problem voiced, 1: 'Help, Lord';
- their problem solved, 7–8, not by a change of circumstances, but by a new conviction and perspective, leading to a new confidence in God.

SIGNPOST: The world is a very noisy place. Days are full of words, let alone other sounds – mine, others', the words of newspapers, books, the media. Many words are worthless. The advertisers, politicians and powerful constantly promise much and then fail to deliver. The words of celebrities are often full of fantasy. Which words I pay attention to matters, as they shape my worldview. Whose words do I listen to as my guide? Do I fight hard enough through the plethora of other voices to listen to the voice of God? Have I space in the day and in my mind to listen to him? And what about the words I speak? How do they measure up in the light of verses such as Prov. 10:19; 12:18; 13:3; 15:4, 23; 16:24; 18:13; 20:15 and 25:11?

Economical with the truth

 ORIENTATION: Impatient with God because of your circumstances? Then this short prayer that begins in desperation but moves through prayer to restoration is for you. We do not know the circumstances that caused it to be written, which means we can claim it whenever circumstances make us think God is hiding from us (v. 1).

MAP: This psalm charts a clear route to progress.

A cry of desperation: the problem stated, 1–2
The psalmist protests:
- my God has forgotten me, 1;
- my mind is tormenting me, 2;
- my enemies are attacking me, 2b.

A cry for transformation: the problem staunched, 3–4
The prayer is addressed to 'Lord my God', the name that highlights God's covenant relationship (see p. 46) with his people. Because of their covenant commitment, the psalmist's destiny is tied up with God's honour. So the problem begins to be answered as he prays:
- positively, 3: restore my life;
- negatively, 4: defeat my enemies.

A cry of expectation: the problem solved, 5–6
Having prayed, rather than continuing in negative depression, the psalmist discovers a new vitality in life because he:
- trusts in God's love, 5a;
- hopes in God's salvation, 5b;
- rejoices in God's providence, 6.

SIGNPOST: The instant society in which I live may compound the problem, but I am impatient by temperament. I can identify with David's impatience as he raises the question 'How long?' four times in vv. 1–2. I have often wanted God to bring the waiting to an end, the agony to a close and the suspense to a conclusion. Like David in vv. 3–4, I have pressed God for a resolution to some-one's prolonged illness, a job uncertainty, or an awkward situation. But God knows what he is doing. His timing serves a purpose and is better than mine. I need to cultivate the patient trust of vv. 5–6, trust that does not arise from mere resignation, but perseveres as an active hope in God's goodness. Heb. 6:12 instructs us 'to imitate those who through faith and patience inherit what has been promised'.

Psalm 14 ✓

 ORIENTATION: This is a reflective psalm in the wisdom tradition, rather than a rant. It concerns the effects of practical atheism and tempts one to ask the question, 'Does God believe in atheists?' The word 'fools' here describes not so much the ignorant as the arrogant. It describes those who are wicked rather than stupid.

MAP: Drawn from a high altitude, this psalm presents an overview of:

The foolish denial of God, 1, 4

Their folly:

- stems from human arrogance, 1a;
- leads to wrongful behaviour, 1b: why bother if there is no God?
- results in social division and community breakdown, 4.

The beneficial reality of God, 2–3, 5–7

Whatever practical atheists think, it is beneficial to believe in God because:

- God reigns, 2, 'from heaven';
- God recognizes, 2–3, how few seek him;
- God resides, 5, among his people;
- God rescues, 6, 'the poor';
- God restores, 7, the community.

Here are grounds not only for believing in God, but also for rejoicing in him.

LINKS: Psalm 53 virtually repeats this psalm.

SIGNPOST: Christine was a keen follower of Jesus with a faith sustained by her youth group until she went to work in a large office where no-one else seemed to believe. Her faith began to struggle and, sadly, eventually to wither and die. Christian believers are often a tiny island surrounded by an ocean of unbelievers, at least in the Western world. Faith calls us *to believe against* what the majority think as much as *to believe in* God. Does this psalm help us do that by showing what sort of society is created by those who don't see themselves as accountable to God? Is that borne out in our experience? Do we see the wisdom of believing, not just for ourselves, but for our communities, and does that strengthen our faith?

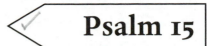

 ORIENTATION: Although the title claims this as a psalm of David, it is most likely to have been sung by pilgrims visiting Jerusalem. It begins with a question that strangers to Jerusalem were likely to ask. Who is fit to enter God's presence? Who is permitted to enter the temple? Most of the psalm provides the answer before ending with a promise.

MAP: Directions for entering the temple include:

Conditions, 2

Those who enter God's presence must be:
- blameless: not perfect, but wholehearted in their desire to please God;
- righteous: in relation to their neighbours;
- truthful: in speech and relationships.

Prohibitions, 3–5

They must not:
- harm their neighbours, 3: the community dimension;
- encourage the wicked, 4a: the moral dimension;
- despise the godly, 4b: the religious dimension;
- manipulate the market, 4c, 5: the commercial dimension;
- exploit the poor, 5a: the social dimension.

LINKS: The ten qualities mentioned in vv. 2–5 have been compared with the Ten Commandments. They 'put flesh on' the godly who are commended in Psalm 1:1–3 and stand in contrast to the ungodly of Psalm 1:4–6, who are then described further in Psalm 14. Is such perfection possible? Possibly not. This is about intention, not achievement. 2 Pet. 1:5–9 is a suitable commentary on this. The promise is that such people 'will never be shaken' (v. 5).

SIGNPOST: Many elderly saints whose long pilgrimage has honed their characters over many years exemplify this psalm. We should thank God for them. But what is it that makes them attractive? I must ask myself what it means to live a blameless life. The psalm seems to measure it by how we live in our everyday lives as neighbours and citizens rather than how we act as worshippers. What happens outside the temple determines who gets admitted. It leads me to wonder if my Christianity is measured too much by religion – that is, by how I act in church and what I think about 'church issues' – and not enough by how I live in the 'real' world.

'The Maker of heaven and earth'

Five times the Psalms call God 'the Maker of heaven and earth' (115:15; 121:2; 124:8; 134:3; 146:6). Planet earth and its surrounding universe came into existence by the conscious decision and action of God, not by accident, chance or the outworking of impersonal forces. And that, say the Psalms, is something worth celebrating.

Songs of creation are scattered throughout the book (see, e.g., 8, 19, 29, 33, 104, 145). Obvious joy is taken in the beauty and majesty of creation. The earth, sea and air, the heights and the depths, the variety of its creatures, the diversity of its weather, the sufficiency of its resources and the dependability of its times and seasons all call for comment. The immensity of the heavens is contrasted with the minuscule nature of human beings, and yet it is humans who are the pinnacle of God's creation (8:3–8).

The psalmists may have been more alert to the wonder of creation because they lived more closely in touch with it. Many of us live in an urban, humanly constructed and technological environment, sheltered from the rawness of nature. But the psalmists had little to cushion them from immediately experiencing God's creation.

Creation itself is never worshipped. The focus is always on the Lord of creation whose name is majestic in all the earth (8:1, 9). He reveals himself in his creation (19:1–6) as well as in his law (19:7–14). What we encounter is a God of power who created the world by his word (33:6, 9; 65:5–8; 148:5–6). The stars respond to his command as he names them (147:4). His wisdom led him to create (104:25–26; 136:5–9). And having made the heavens and the earth, he maintains an active, personal interest and involvement with them (19:1–2; 67:6–7; 85:12; 107:23–38). We dare not take creation for granted. 'Give thanks to the Lord of lords . . . to him who alone does great wonders' (136:3–4).

 ORIENTATION: Here is an unabashed celebration of a relation-ship with God that culminates, in v. 11, with the statement, 'In your presence there is fullness of joy' (NRSV). En route the psalmist finds joy in so much else.

MAP: Everything revolves around God:

The primacy of God, 1–2

God is chosen as the centre of life and is more than sufficient for whatever we may meet in it.

The people of God, 3–4

Loving God leads us to love his people, who, for all their faults, are noble, while idolaters are fools.

The provision of God, 5–6

We should be thankful and not guilty when our 'boundary lines have fallen . . . in pleasant places'. This is life as God intended for his creation.

The providence of God, 7

He proves a wise guide for every circumstance and I am wise if I immerse myself in his words so deeply that they work on my self-conscious even when I am asleep.

The protection of God, 8

Listening to his instruction leads to security.

The presence of God, 9–11

The psalmist rejects the contemporary view that all is emptiness after death and believes that death will give way to a richer, fuller life in God's presence. This resurrection hope is quoted in Acts 2:25–28 and 13:35.

SIGNPOST: My grandmother was bombed out of her house three times during World War II, losing virtually everything, yet she would testify that vv. 5–11 of this psalm are true. In fact, it was her favourite psalm. She not only loved this psalm, but lived it. She and other saints of her generation immersed themselves in Scripture, in prayer and in Christian fellowship. They saw God protect and lead them. James Mays said of this psalm, 'The Lord fills the personal horizon of the psalmist. Every one of the prayer's lines in all their variety says in one way or another, "The Lord is everything to me." The Lord is my lord, my God, my destiny, my counsel, my vis-à-vis, my security. The whole confesses, "The Lord is my life."' Could I say the same?

ORIENTATION: Forged in the heat of trouble (vv. 9–14), this psalm, like the previous one, also rejoices in a secure relationship with God. The psalmist is aware of 'the wonders of your great love' (v. 7) and prays that God would keep him 'as the apple of your eye' (v. 8).

 MAP: He asks God to:

Hear me, 1–2

Three times the psalmist asks God to hear him. His quest is urgent.

Test me, 3–5

As often, the psalmist is concerned to establish his integrity and ensure he has not caused his suffering by his sin. It is a claim not to sinless perfection, but to innocence in the face of false accusations.

Love me, 6–9

This is about more than mere rescue. The warmth and fine expression of a loving relationship here is based on the covenant agreement God has with his people.

Save me, 10–14

The psalmist needs the Lord to step in to rescue him and deal with the wicked who oppose him.

Keep me, 15

' . . . until this is all over and then I'll wake from the nightmare and be satisfied, again, with you.'

SIGNPOST: What strikes me in this psalm is the affection David shows for God and the tenderness he expects, for good reason, to find in God. 'The apple of your eye' (v. 8) refers to a very tender part of the eye and has come to signify a very special relationship between people. The verse conjures up the image of a young child with her mother in the first line and a young bird with its mother in the second. What a contrast to the harsh, unforgiving world in which we live. And what a contrast to the harsh, unforgiving picture of God many have. I can thank God for the tenderness he has shown me when as a weak spiritual child I have needed it and as a wayward child I have not deserved it.

Psalm 18

ORIENTATION: The above title for this lengthy psalm comes from *The Message*'s translation of v. 28. (Eugene Peterson provides a brilliant translation of Psalm 18 in *The Message*.) It explains why the psalmist can begin by talking not of his fear of God, nor of his mere obedience to God, but of his love for God.

MAP: In charting salvation, the psalm speaks of:

The God of salvation, 1–2
A multitude of images pour out in praise.

The need for salvation, 3–6
The psalmist faced death, drowning and destruction.

The source of salvation, 7–15
God steps in – and down from heaven.

The experience of salvation, 16–19
Salvation is seen as rescue, refuge, renewal and romance.

The results of salvation, 20–29
It brings a new commitment, 20–27; new colour, 28; and a new power to life, 29.

The purpose of salvation, 30–45
The psalmist is now armed and trained for battle.

The assurance of salvation, 46–50
It ends with the cry, 'The Lord lives!'

SIGNPOST: The images come thick and fast here, including two of my favourite pictures of salvation. The first is that of the rock (v. 2) and the second that of a spacious place (v. 19). Walking on the sand one day, I was unexpectedly caught in a patch of quicksand and felt myself being sucked in. It wasn't life-threatening, but suddenly to have nothing firm under one's feet was scary. What a relief to place your feet on a rock that won't give way. Then, having lived for some years in a grey-walled and rainy city, what deliverance it was to leave the confines of that city behind and get out to a spacious moor where I could breathe and live again. What is your favourite image of salvation in the psalm and why?

God floodlights my life

Psalm 19 ✓

 ORIENTATION: We live in a communication age, but our God has been in the communication business from the beginning of time. It is in his nature to communicate with the people he has made.

 MAP: Three forms of his communication are mentioned here:

The silent voice of God, 1–6

In creation God makes himself known, speaking through:

- the skies, 1;
- the silence, 2–4b;
- the sun, 4c–6.

The written voice of God, 7–11

God also communicates through the law. The psalmist notes:

- its varied forms, 7–9: laws, precepts, commands, etc.;
- its immense value, 10: it is 'more precious than gold';
- its beneficial effects, 7–11: in giving refreshment, wisdom, insight, joy and warning;
- its utter reliability, 7–9: it is 'perfect', 'trustworthy', 'right', 'pure', 'enduring' and 'sure'.

The penetrating voice of God, 12–14

C. S. Lewis commented that in this psalm, 'the searching and cleansing sun becomes an image of the searching and cleansing law':

- it makes us aware of sin;
- it leads us to ask for help;
- it gives us a desire to please him.

C. S. Lewis also wrote, 'I take this to be the greatest poem in the Psalter and one of the greatest lyrics in the world.'

SIGNPOST: Some of us learn best through visual means and some through verbal instruction. Evangelicalism has sometimes been excessively verbal. The psalmist caters for both here and says that God uses both to make himself known. How much can I learn of God from observation rather than from listening or reading? I note the connection the psalm makes between 'these words of my mouth and this meditation of my heart' (v. 14). Am I careful enough in choosing what I watch, look at and read? In other words, am I discerning enough about what occupies my mind ('heart')? Look at Paul's advice in Phil. 4:8–9.

 **ORIENTATION**: Although the specific situation is unknown, this seems to be a prayer psalm sung on the eve of battle. It looks to God to answer (vv. 1, 9) the needs of the unnamed king.

MAP: 'The name of the Lord' is mentioned three times in this psalm (vv. 1b, 5b, 7).

The name of the Lord provides protection, 1–3
The people pray to the ageless covenant God of Jacob for:

- safety from harm, 2a;
- strength to cope, 2b;
- acceptance of sacrifices, 3.

The name of the Lord promises victory, 4–5
They continue to pray in faith and anticipation for:

- the fulfilment of the king's plans, 4;
- the celebration of the Lord's victory, 5.

The name of the Lord proves trustworthy, 6–9
With intensifying conviction, an individual responds confidently, saying, 'I know':

- God's power will be evident, 6;
- God's ways must be trusted, 7; and consequently,
- God's people can be steadfast, 8.

SIGNPOST: What's in a name? The answer is, an awful lot. A hippy-looking student of mine once appeared at the gate of a military barracks and was about to be smartly turned away until he said his name. His father was the CO! He was promptly admitted with a salute. How much more wonderful is the name of God. Moreover, unlike the psalmist, we know the name of Jesus, 'the name that is above every name' and the one to which one day every knee should bow (Phil. 2:9–10). His name promises victory over all our enemies and total salvation. It is always a name that can be trusted and will never let us down.

The God who saves me

The theme of salvation drips through the Psalms like hot water filtering through gauze to distil into a rich aromatic cup of coffee. God is often described as 'the God who saves me' (51:14; 55:16; 68:20; 88:1) and even more often simply as 'Saviour' (e.g., 18:46; 25:5; 27:9; 38:22; 42:11; 68:19; 85:4; 89:26). Some psalms pray to God for salvation and others celebrate a salvation already received from him. Salvation is deliverance.

Salvation is both spiritual and material. There are times when the deliverance sought is from sin and its consequences, as in Psalm 51. But more often the psalmist looks to be rescued from sickness, either of a physical or an emotional kind (22, 38, 42), from enemy attacks (7, 18, 60, 79, 106), or from the unnamed troubles of ordinary life (34, 54, 107).

Salvation is both personal and national. The prayers and praises of salvation are both intensely personal (17, 31, 69, 86) and grandly national (28, 60, 106, 108). God is concerned as much with the fate of the individual 'me' as with the covenant 'we'.

Salvation is available to all who need it. Sometimes salvation seems preferentially available to those in a close relationship with God (20:6; 37:39; 86:16). However, the truth is that it is available to all, from the king (20:9) downwards. God is especially concerned to rescue those who are unable to rescue themselves, namely the vulnerable (72:4, 13; 82:3–4; 107:41; 113:7–9) and broken-hearted (34:8).

Salvation and judgment go together, two sides of the same coin. The deliverance of the one in need necessarily involves judgment on what-ever or whomever has caused the oppression. Vindication of the innocent inevitably involves the condemnation of the guilty (31, 53, 76, 79, 94).

Salvation is unique to him. The living God of Israel alone has the power to rescue people from their oppression. His ability to deliver people stands in sharp contrast to 'worthless idols' (31:6; 97:7) or even human resources and weapons (20:7; 44:6; 49:6; 118:8–9). 'He alone is my rock and my salvation' (62:2, 6).

 ORIENTATION: This has much in common with the previous psalm, but while that psalm prayed for victory in the future, this psalm celebrates a victory that has been granted. This is a royal psalm that rejoices in the strength God gives.

MAP: A simple map draws attention to the psalm's two halves:

Past blessings, 1–7
Among the blessings of the past, the psalmist rejoices in:
- God's strength, 1;
- answered prayer, 2;
- royal status, 3;
- long life, 4;
- many victories, 5;
- God's presence, 6;
- unfailing love, 7.

Future victories, 8–12
A whole variety of expressions are used to describe the success the people expect the king to have in future battles and the ease with which his enemies will be eliminated. Yet the victories are not because of the king's skill, but because of the Lord's power (v. 9).

LINKS: Verses 1 and 13 celebrate the Lord's strength. The psalm finds its fulfilment in Jesus, who is King of kings. Spurgeon commented, 'Herein let every subject imitate the King; let us lean upon Jehovah's strength . . .'

SIGNPOST: A friend used to keep a diary in which he would record at least one thing for which he was thankful every day. After one miserable day when everything had gone wrong, all he could think to record was his thankfulness that the day was over. In Psalm 20 they pray for victory. In Psalm 21 they give thanks for the prayer having been answered positively. How often do we pray and then forget to thank God when the answer comes? What steps do we take to ensure that we practise the spiritual discipline of thanksgiving? Do we, in the quaint words of the old hymn, 'Count (our) blessings, name them one by one'?

Psalm 22 ✓

 ORIENTATION: Christ's anguished cry of desertion on the cross (Mark 15:33) comes from the first verse of this psalm. The psalm asks, 'Where is God when it hurts?'

MAP: This intricately crafted psalm interweaves trouble and trust, but ends in transformation.

The trouble he faces, 1–2, 6–8, 12–18
The psalmist:

- longs for God, 1–2;
- is loathed by others, 6–8;
- laments for himself, 12–18.

The trust he shows, 3–5, 9–11, 19–21
He affirms:

- God's position, 3: 'enthroned';
- God's power, 4–5: 'they cried . . . you . . . saved';
- God's purpose, 9: God did not bring him to birth for nothing;
- God's providence, 10–11: God has protected him since his birth;
- God's person, 19–21: his strength and his saviour.

The transformation he experiences, 22–31
The psalmist promises that when he recovers:

- he will express public praise, 22–26;
- he will dream a universal vision, 27–31.

SIGNPOST: Children quickly protest, 'Why me?' when they get any whiff of unfairness. But as adults most of us will have cried, 'Why me, Lord?' on occasions. The question was voiced most profoundly when Jesus cried from the cross, 'My God, my God, why have you forsaken me?' What did he mean? Some say he had expected to be delivered by God before ending up dead, but that God had let him down. Others say it's a natural cry of anguish from a son who felt deserted by his father in his moment of need. All it is, they say, is raw emotion, since God could not desert his Son because the relationship of the Trinity cannot be broken. Others rightly say there was a real separation between Father and Son because on the cross the Son bore the world's sin (2 Cor. 5:21) and God is inherently too pure even to look on evil (Hab. 1:13). Anything less than this would not be sufficient to secure our salvation. But the separation was soon overcome by the strength of the loving bond between Father and Son, as the resurrection shows.

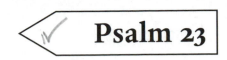
 ORIENTATION: It may be foolish, pretentious and unnecessary to comment on this psalm, which is better known than any other. It speaks of God as shepherd (vv. 1–2), travelling companion (vv. 3–4) and host (vv. 5–6). It begins and ends with the Lord and has an emphatic 'you' in v. 4. And yet it is full of 'I' and 'me' and 'my'. It should be read against the background of a shepherd's journeying in the wilderness, of which David would have plenty of personal experience. It testifies to the fact that 'life with Yahweh is a life of well-being and satisfaction' (Brueggemann).

MAP: One map might be as follows:

The Lord is my owner, 1a: he is 'my shepherd'.

The Lord is my provider, 1b: 'I lack nothing'.

The Lord is my refreshment, 2–3a: in the barren desert.

The Lord is my guide, 3: he directs me when the way is not clear.

The Lord is my companion, 4: there is a realism about problems and suffering, but they are transformed by God's presence.

The Lord is my instructor, 4b: the rod and staff were used to ward off wild animals, but also to teach sheep and bring them back into line.

The Lord is my host, 5–6: the final picture is one of secure abundance.

SIGNPOST: A friend of mine, a confident and loquacious evangelist, once struggled to find any words at all. It was in 1966 when he was conducting the funeral of some of the 116 children and 28 adults killed in Aberfan, where a coal tip had collapsed and buried them alive in their school. He said, 'All I could do through the tears was read Psalm 23 and emphasize, "Even though I walk *through* the valley of the shadow of death, I will fear no evil, for thou art with me." That was enough.' This psalm has spoken to millions in a multitude of circumstances, but especially in situations of stress, danger and grief – situations like those of a barren desert. What phrase has particularly spoken to you, or what image have you found particularly helpful in this psalm?

ORIENTATION: This psalm conjures up the picture of a procession. The statement (vv. 1–2), question (vv. 3–6) and command (vv. 7–10) here all relate to it. It may have been written for the procession bringing the ark to Jerusalem, recorded in 1 Chr. 16, but it might also have in mind the journey of the children of Israel from Egypt to Jerusalem, which was quite a procession!

MAP: The psalm captures different aspects of the procession:

The start of the procession, 1–2
The procession is not just through a few local streets, but starts far away, because it involves God and he is *the Lord of the whole earth.*

The participants in the procession, 3–6
The key question is, who has a right to enter the city or temple with the King? The answer is, those who are inwardly as well as outwardly clean. That is what it means to seek him. Verse 5 stresses blessing as God's gift, because he is *the God of amazing grace.*

The focus of the procession, 7–10
The arrival of the mighty warrior is celebrated with the doors, metaphorically, being told to make room for him as he enters the city / temple. This is because *he is the King of majestic glory.*

SIGNPOST: The accession of Queen Elizabeth II brought millions out onto the streets of Britain, not only on the drizzly Coronation Day itself in London in 1953, but subsequently up and down the country as she toured her new realm. I stood enthusiastically waving a flag with the rest of my class of new school entrants to greet her grand cavalcade as she swept through our little town. We were scrubbed clean and dressed smartly to greet the young woman who had been given all sorts of titles at her recent enthronement. How much more care should we exercise in greeting the King of glory, the Lord Almighty, who is no mere constitutional monarch and whose titles are anything but fictitious?

ORIENTATION: Verse 14 is the key to this psalm. It somewhat curiously says, 'The friendship of the Lord is for those who fear him' (NRSV). We don't normally associate friendship and fear, but reverence and respect are indispensable if we are to enjoy friendship with God. It is a wisdom psalm that develops the theme of Psalm 1 and Prov. 1:7 with its message about practical godliness.

MAP: The psalm roughly falls into two halves:

The meaning of fear, 1–10

To fear God means to:

- actively trust in him, 1–3;
- take direction from him, 4–5;
- seek mercy from him, 6–7 (see also, 11, 18b);
- acquire humility before him, 9;
- live obediently under him, 10;
- maintain focus on him, 5c, 15a.

The meaning of friendship, 10–20

Friendship with God leads us to experience his:

- faithfulness instead of fickleness, 10: his love is constant;
- pardon instead of sinfulness, 11: his grace is abundant;
- direction instead of uncertainty, 12–14: his guidance is trustworthy;
- protection instead of trials, 15: his deliverance is assured;
- companionship instead of loneliness, 16: his presence is comforting;
- relief instead of trouble, 17–20: his salvation is all-embracing.

LINKS: Abraham (Isa. 41:8; Jas 2:23) was called God's friend. James contrasts friendship with the world with that of God in 4:4–10.

SIGNPOST: 'He was fine until he fell in with the wrong kind of friends and now he won't listen to a word I say.' Andy's mother was explaining her exasperation with him to me after he had been caught stealing from the collection plate. Friends have a powerful impact on us, for good or ill. That's why Prov. 13:20 admonishes, 'Walk with the wise and become wise, for a companion of fools suffers harm.' Friendship with God is the best of all. Like any true human friendship, it develops out of a commitment to each other and to common outlooks and interests. Friendship with God can never be a friendship of equals, but it can be genuine nonetheless, providing we give ourselves to live in a way that pleases him.

The friendship of the Lord

Covenant love

Underlying many of the psalms is the idea of covenant, an agreement binding two parties in a relationship. Covenants are both more personal and more comprehensive than contracts. Ancient sovereign powers entered into covenants with subject people. In like manner, God covenants himself to be Israel's God and Israel to be his special people.

Covenants are found in the stories of Noah and Abraham. Through Moses, God entered into the covenant with Israel as a whole that is described in Exod. 34, Lev. 26 and Deut. 29 – 30, together with the blessings that Israel will experience if they keep their side of it by obeying his law (happiness, guidance, protection, peace and prosperity) and the disasters ('curses') that will come their way in increasing magnitude if they do not.

The core of God's blessing is his love. Covenant love is strong, unfailing, faithful and enduring. *Hesed*, the Hebrew word for it, crops up frequently. Indeed, about half the Old Testament occurrences are to be found here. It speaks of God's deep commitment to Israel and his willingness to give himself on their behalf. Several psalms express unqualified joy for this love (16, 34, 91, 103, 136). It is patient love, but it can be misleading to say it's 'unconditional love', since it requires Israel to obey the covenant. But it always wins through in the end (Ps. 25:10)

Special interest is shown in the covenant with David (2 Sam. 7) and his dynasty. The 'royal psalms' celebrate this (2, 18, 20, 45, 89, 110) and breathe an air of confidence about the security of his throne, the certainty of the victories and the permanence of Jerusalem and the temple (46, 48, 84). But David's successors broke the covenant with the result that Israel lost God's protection and went into exile. The psalms forged by that experience express confession, bewilderment, or simply lament about their situation. Some look to restoration in the future (74, 79, 85, 89, 126, 132, 137).

Individuals are embraced by God's covenant with the nation and some very personal psalms express that relationship in all its ups and downs (17, 22, 25, 32, 77, 103).

Covenant defined the relationship between God and Israel, just as the new covenant (Jer. 33; 2 Cor. 3:7–18; Heb. 7:22) defines the relationship between God and Christians today.

ORIENTATION: Trouble again! This time the trouble arises from false accusations. The psalmist protests his innocence.

 MAP: David is:

Pleading his cause, 1–3
The psalmist:

- protests his 'integrity' (see NLT): he is not claiming sinless perfection, but rather wholeheartedness in following God;
- proclaims his trust, 1b: the basis for his hope;
- submits to examination, 2–3, seeking no favours.

Presenting his evidence, 4–8

- The evidence is negative, 4–5: he has not associated with the wicked.
- The evidence is positive, 6–8: he has enjoyed God's presence in the temple.

Protesting his innocence, 9–12
These verses read like a final statement before a jury, summing up his case. He does not claim perfection in v. 11, but wholehearted commitment to God.

In spite of the assaults, the psalmist is still standing (v. 12) and rejects cynicism and bitterness. Throughout, he knows the outcome lies in the Lord's hands.

SIGNPOST: There are times when mere survival is a great achievement. Jan Burn suddenly faced the challenge of her son being diagnosed with a life-threatening cancer and undergoing prolonged and distressing treatment. The emotional and spiritual pressures, already enormous, were aggravated by the expectations people had of her as a church leader. But she, and he, came through. The moving story is told with raw honesty in *I'm Still Standing* (BRF, 2005) and reveals how often the Psalms came to her aid. Elton John's 'I'm Still Standing' became their song at the time. Verse 12 testifies to something similar. Are there times when we, or others, are under such fierce attack that to keep standing on level ground is a great triumph? Are we sometimes unrealistic in our expectations of those under great pressure, assault or false accusation?

Declare me innocent

Psalm 27 ✓

 ORIENTATION: This psalm goes through the whole spectrum of emotion, from confidence to desperation. But Brueggemann believes, 'Confidence wins out over trouble.'

 MAP: The psalm is composed of four elements.

His declaration, 1–3

Verses 2–3 explain the reason for him declaring his faith in v. 1.

His dedication, 4–6

His dedication to God is seen in:

- his focus, 4a: 'one thing I ask';
- his passion, 4b: 'this only do I seek';
- his desire, 4b–c, to delight 'in the Lord's perfections' (NLT): God's perfections are worth considering;
- his faithfulness, 5–6, to go on trusting in trouble.

His determination, 7–10

He is determined to find God and not be left abandoned. Although this is not easy, he's convinced God will prove faithful when others let him down.

His destination, 11–14

On the journey to seeing God coming to his defence again:

- he seeks guidance, 11;
- he acknowledges obstacles, 11b–12;
- he exudes confidence, 13;
- he waits patiently, 14.

LINKS: Jesus said, 'I am the light of the world' (John 8:12).

SIGNPOST: David's one desire is to 'gaze on the beauty of the Lord', which means that which is excellent and desirable in him. Earlier generations referred to it as 'the perfections of God', which include his eternity, majesty, holiness, wisdom, goodness, justice, love, grace, truth, unchangeableness, omniscience, omnipresence and omnipotence. I am an activist and too busy to stop and gaze: a quick glimpse has to suffice! It's partly temperament and personality. Yet temperaments need refining and there's wisdom in lingering over some scenes. Sitting by a lake, gazing at the ocean, or viewing an expanse from on high is highly refreshing. So wouldn't I find contemplating God's beauty spiritually refreshing? Wouldn't it give me more depth in my relationship with him?

The Lord is my light

ORIENTATION: This further prayer for help is full of imagery about God. It begins with the Lord being described as 'my Rock', a frequent image found in 18:2, 31, 46; 19:14, etc., and moves through a phase of uncertainty (vv. 3–5) before ending on a very positive note. Verses 7–9, however, contain a concentration of images that relate to the psalmist individually and to the community as a whole.

MAP: In vv. 7–9 God serves as:

The strong one who supports, 7: 'The Lord is my strength';

The shield who protects, 7: 'and my shield';

The song that gladdens, 7: 'with my song I praise him';

The saviour who rescues, 8: 'a fortress of salvation';

The shepherd who guides, 9: 'be their shepherd';

The sustainer who carries, 9: 'and carry them for ever'.

SIGNPOST: In his psalms David uses positive images to describe God that arise from the world in which he lived. Some reflect the military situation – 'shield', 'fortress'; some the workaday world of the shepherd; others the more personal and social context of romance or sitting around the camp fire and singing. What images of our world might describe God in positive terms? A global space defence shield, a nurse in a hospice, an eternal and never-failing internet, a divine iPod, or what?

Psalm 29 ✓

 ORIENTATION: The first verse of the hymn 'How Great Thou Art' speaks of the 'awesome wonder' of God's creation and especially of his power displayed in hearing 'the mighty thunder'. The same sentiment occurs here as the psalmist reflects on the God of the storm. The language of 'heavenly beings' in v. 1 comes from the Canaanites, as does the idea of the high God holding court.

MAP: Giving directions about worship, we read of:

The summons to worship, 1–2
The 'heavenly beings' are called to worship God for 'the splendour of his holiness' – that is, for what he is.

The substance of worship, 3–9
Seven times the psalm speaks of 'the voice of the Lord', describing the path and the effects of a storm. His voice is 'powerful', 'majestic'. It 'breaks', 'shakes', 'strikes', 'twists' and 'strips' trees in the forest. God's voice both causes havoc and triumphs over chaos. It provokes worship.

The solace of worship, 10–11
God is eternally ('for ever') sovereign ('enthroned') over all chaos and graciously 'blesses his people with peace'.

SIGNPOST: On the night before David Jenkins was due to be consecrated as Bishop of Durham in York Minster in 1984, lightning struck the Minister, setting part of the roof on fire. David Jenkins's appointment was controversial, for he was understood as having denied the orthodox view of the resurrection of Christ. The interesting thing was to see both archbishops on breakfast TV denying (a) that God could do such a thing and (b) that he would have done it if he could. How different is the psalmist, who hears the voice of God in the thunder and bows in awestruck wonder before the God who engages with his creation in such power. Are we in danger of explaining nature in terms of scientific rationalism so much that we distance God from his world and fail to hear his voice when he rightly claims our attention?

ORIENTATION: This psalm must have been a comfort to countless thousands, especially when facing bereavement. After weeping comes 'rejoicing in the morning'. Sorrow passes and a new day begins. Verse 11 bears witness to God's transforming abilities in the worst of situations to turn 'wailing into dancing' in this life. The psalm demonstrates a resolute, determined faith. No matter what we face in the present, joy will come.

MAP: Against the background of God's permissive discipline, we read of:

The healing God brings, 1–3: the psalmist is brought back from near death;

The joy God gives, 4–5: weeping is real, but does not last;

The security God provides, 6–7: there is a danger in taking it for granted and so being unprepared and unable to cope when trouble comes;

The future God opens, 8–10: the psalmist points out that there is no value to be gained by his death;

The change God works, 11–12: from wailing to dancing.

LINKS: Verse 5b has something of the flavour of 2 Cor. 4:17 and Rom. 8:18.

SIGNPOST: Grace had lived a comfortable life when, without warning, disaster struck. Her husband unexpectedly died while they were on holiday abroad and then it came out that he had been involved, unknown to her, in a number of shady financial deals. So, just as she was coping with bereavement, she learned that she was also going to lose her house, her car and most of her possessions. Naturally she shed a good many tears. But when I met her a year or so later, she had recovered her joy in God and testified to the many ways he had provided for her throughout her nightmare, and the life he had restored to her. She didn't blame God, but rather had a deeper appreciation of the value of trusting him. Psalm 30 was her psalm!

God's activity in history

The faith of the children of Israel was not a fiction, the invention of their own pious imagination. It was a faith built on the evidence of God at work in their experience. The Psalms are not abstract theology, but thoroughly rooted in the history of Israel. When they refer to their history, they do so in a way that is consistent with the story as told elsewhere, even if they bring their own particular perspective to it. One feature is that although important figures in history, such as Moses, are mentioned, the spotlight falls on God, who is said to have caused the events they celebrate.

A few psalms (68, 78, 105, 106) are big-picture psalms. They tell the grand story, usually to encourage Israel to learn from history and not repeat the mistakes of the past. They provide 'a theological compass for the future' (Bullock). Others mention one or another episode in Israel's history.

The story of oppression in Egypt and the events surrounding the exodus are frequently retold (66, 68, 78, 80, 81, 105, 106, 114, 135, 136). Psalm 66:5–6 characteristically says that God arranged it. 'Come and see what God has done, his awesome deeds for humankind! He turned the sea into dry land, they passed through the waters on foot – come, let us rejoice in him.'

The giving of the law in Sinai and the journey through the wilderness are particularly mentioned in the big-picture psalms. The conquest of the land comes up in 44, 80 and 114, among others. The period of the monarchy is celebrated. The royal psalms speak of God establishing David on the throne (see especially 78:70–72) and of 'the David covenant as the still point in a turning world' (Bullock). But the still point was soon to be thrown into confusion and other psalms take up the exile and restoration as their subjects (106, 107, 126, 137).

The God of Israel is a God who made himself known through past events and continues to reveal himself through present experiences in a way that is consistent with that revelation of his character and his will.

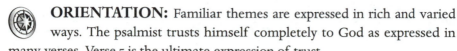

Psalm 31

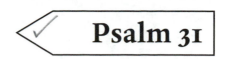

ORIENTATION: Familiar themes are expressed in rich and varied ways. The psalmist trusts himself completely to God as expressed in many verses. Verse 5 is the ultimate expression of trust.

MAP: Perhaps the following picks up the thread of the psalm:

Life is in God's hands when:
- life is in danger, 1–3: 'deliver me';
- testing is near, 4–5: 'keep me free from the trap';
- the soul is in anguish, 6–8: 'the anguish of my soul';
- the body is weak, 9–10: 'my strength fails';
- friends have deserted, 11–13: 'those who see me . . . flee from me';
- lies are told, 14–18: 'let their lying lips be silenced';
- the future is uncertain, 19–20: 'stored up';
- rejection is felt, 21–22: 'I am cut off from your sight';
- and, conversely, praise is easy, 23–24: 'Love the Lord, all his faithful people'.

Phrases worth meditating on

There are so many wonderful phrases here worth reflecting on in the presence of God: 'Be my rock of refuge' (v. 2); 'into your hands . . . ' (v. 5); 'worthless idols' (v. 6); 'a spacious place' (v. 8); 'be merciful to me' (v. 9); 'you are my God' (v. 14); 'my times are in your hands' (v. 15); 'how great is your goodness' (v. 19); 'the shelter of your presence' (v. 20); 'be strong and take heart' (v. 24).

LINKS: Jesus quoted v. 5 in his dying breath (Luke 23:46).

SIGNPOST: It's easy to see our lives being in God's hands (v. 15) when things are going well, but not so easy when we encounter difficulties. This psalm ranges over the varied situations that make life precarious. It can be used as a prayer agenda for those facing trouble. Pray for those who face death (vv. 1–3); strong temptation (vv. 4–5); spiritual turmoil (vv. 6–8); failing health (vv. 9–10); loneliness (vv. 11–13); persecution (vv. 14–18); uncertain futures (vv. 19–20); rejection by God (vv. 21–22). Equally rejoice with those who know God's goodness (vv. 23–24). Pray that they may experience the truths asserted in the psalm.

My life in God's hands

Psalm 32 ✓>

 ORIENTATION: With Psalm 51, this is one of the great penitential psalms, where sin and its effects are confronted. Yet the phrase that stands out is in v. 7: 'You are my hiding place; you will protect me from trouble.' The *Living Bible* translated it, 'You are my hiding place from every storm of life.'

MAP: The psalm speaks of:

- relief when sins are confessed, 1–7;
- recovery when God is our guide, 8–9;
- rejoicing when hearts are pure, 10–11.

Note also:

God is:

- a hiding place from guilt, 1–6; Isa. 53:4–6;
- a hiding place in suffering; Isa. 43:2;
- a hiding place in temptation; 1 Cor. 10:13;
- a hiding place in change; Mal. 3:6; Heb. 13:8;
- a hiding place in loneliness; Prov. 18:24; Heb. 13:5.

Important factors in guidance, 8–9

- We can depend on God's promise: 'I will'.
- We can trust to God's providence: 'with my loving eye on you'.
- We can realize God's purpose – to make us fully human, not animals that have to be tightly or mechanically controlled.

SIGNPOST: During World War II, many Jewish families were courageously, and safely, hidden from the Gestapo by Gentile families. A Dutch Christian family from Haarlem called ten Boom provided shelter for many fugitives, but were eventually betrayed and imprisoned. The daughters, Betsie and Corrie, were sent to Ravensbrück, where Betsie died. Throughout their ordeal they maintained a strong faith in Christ and after the war Corrie became an irrepressible evangelist, spreading a message of forgiveness. A book and a film tell the story of her life under the title *The Hiding Place*. They not only provided a hiding place for others, but found the Lord to be a hiding place in Ravensbrück themselves, just as Psalm 32 promises.

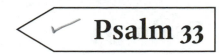

ORIENTATION: Unlike some modern worship leaders, the psalmist not only invites people to sing joyfully (and play skilfully), but lists the reasons why they should do so. His invitation is not an empty command, but rich in explaining why it is 'fitting for the upright to praise him' (v. 1). In spite of such a positive beginning and wonderful content in the middle, the psalm is not triumphalist and ends with a more modest invitation to wait on and hope in God.

MAP: The invitation to sing (vv. 1–3) is issued because:

God's word is truthful, 4–5: his word is 'right and true';

God's work is creative, 6–9: by his word creation was born;

God's will is sovereign, 10–11: his plans 'stand firm';

God's watch is attentive, 12–15: 'he looks down and sees . . . he watches';

God's ways are unconventional, 16–19: he doesn't deliver by armies.

This is enough to keep hope alive and the heart singing, even when circumstances would suggest otherwise.

SIGNPOST: Without wishing to be too negative, what we often experience in society is, at almost every point, the mirror opposite of what this psalm claims about God. We meet with lies, promises that are not kept and advice that is based on ignorance. Words hurt and destroy rather than bring life. The plans, even of government and big business, change, even after they have invested millions in research before agreeing them. People don't look out for each other. And we rely on force and conventional weapons to enforce our will on others. Living like this doesn't create a society at ease with itself or with others. How different is our God? How much better are his ways? Doesn't it make you want to sing that he's the one in ultimate control?

Sing joyfully because . . .

Tasting the Lord's goodness

 ORIENTATION: Apparently written when David was on the run from Saul and after his remarkable escape from King Achish (1 Sam. 21:10–15), this poem revels in God's goodness. It is a 'broken acrostic' that reflects the broken pattern of our lives (Motyer). Each section begins with David's own experience, but then broadens out to embrace others.

MAP: God's goodness is seen through the prism of:

Personal testimony, 1–7

David offers:

- an invitation, 1–3: 'Glorify the Lord with me';
- an explanation, 4–6: 'he delivered me';
- a generalization, 7, a first statement of principle concerning 'those who fear him'.

Wisdom teaching, 8–18

Note references to 'the fear of the Lord' (vv. 7, 9, 11), a common wisdom theme (Prov. 1:7). Again there is:

- an invitation, 8–10: 'Taste and see';
- an explanation, 11–14: 'whoever of you loves life . . .'
- a generalization, 15–18, a second statement of principle.

Reflective thought, 19–22

The psalm concludes as David stands back a little and reflects more generally:

- troubles will continue, 19: that's realistic;
- the wicked will be punished, 21: that's certain;
- the Lord will come to the rescue, 19b, 20, 22: that's ongoing.
  Note: God 'delivers', 'protects', 'redeems' and does not condemn those who take 'refuge in him'.

SIGNPOST: David was in a life-threatening situation. That hasn't been my experience as yet, although many have faced it. But I have been in a couple of extreme situations where all I have lived and worked for looked as though they would come to nothing, resulting in depression. It was during those times that the assurance of v. 18, 'The Lord is close to the broken-hearted and saves those who are crushed in spirit', came to mean so much. In my experience the claim is true. Have you known it to be true yourself? Perhaps you've not been there yet, but you'll know those who are there, so why not pray that the Lord will be close to them today.

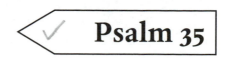

ORIENTATION: Possibly reflecting David's years of running from Saul, this outpouring of lament gives voice to an urgent complaint and bitter tears. Yet trust and thanksgiving are never far below the surface.

MAP: The language of each section suggests a different setting, but each section has the same three elements of pleading, petition and promise. And each ends on a positive note as he vows to praise God.

He seeks victory in the battle, 1–10
- petition, 1–3, using military language: 'fight';
- pleading, 4–8, of his cause and the action sought;
- promise, 9–10, of praising God for his care of the weak.

He seeks deliverance in the jungle, 11–18
- pleading, 11–16, of his cause;
- petition, 17, using jungle language: 'lions';
- promise, 18, of thanksgiving in the congregation.

He seeks vindication in the courtroom, 19–28
- pleading, 19–21, of his cause;
- petition, 22–26, using legal language: 'vindicate';
- promise, 27–28, of witnessing to God's greatness.

LINKS: This is one of the psalms that make us uncomfortable because it expresses David's anger against his enemies: he asks God to bring shame on them and make them like 'chaff before the wind' and deny them hope in the future (vv. 4–6). Other psalms that fall into this group are 55, 59, 69, 79, 109 and 137. For a discussion of the issues they throw up, see the appropriate signposts and the note on 'Psalms of anger' (p. 119).

SIGNPOST: This psalm has the smell of the hunt about it. David is the quarry, his enemies the hunters. Christian leaders in Eastern Europe experienced just that before the fall of the Iron Curtain. Romanian friends of mine could only contact each other in code and travel clandestinely during the worst years of Ceausescu's regime. Occasionally caught by the Securitaté, they knew what it was to be surrounded by lions gnashing their teeth. But they also testify to remarkable deliverances, of the kind David and Peter experienced (Acts 12:1–19). This isn't fiction; it's everyday life for many believers in the world still. How informed are we about them and what can we do to support them?

Thanks through the tears

The Lord reigns

Psalms 47 and 95–99 dwell on the theme of God's reign as 'the great King over all the earth', but many other psalms mention it as well. Indeed, it is the belief that the Lord sits enthroned in the heavens that gives people hope in the face of their troubles on earth (22:3; 29:10; 55:19; 80:1). Being seated so far above the earth doesn't mean he is distant from them or indifferent to their needs. Rather, it suggests he can exercise a careful watch over them, gaining a total picture and a true perspective on life, and as a consequence he is able to administer true justice.

The Lord has reigned from eternity (93:2) and rules now over his creation, being currently in charge of its operation (29:3–10; 50:4; 78:26; 93:1–2; 95:4–6; 96:10–13; 98:7–9). His reign stretches from the past through the present to the future (97:2–7; 98:9).

He rules over people and nations as well as over the physical creation (2:1–12; 22:27–28; 33:10; 47:2–9; 67:4; 99:1–2; 102:15; 117:1). It is asserted as a fact: he does so whether they acknowledge his authority or not. So he rules today as much over Iraq, Saudi Arabia, Indonesia and Sudan as he does over the so-called Christian countries such as America and the UK. The gods worshipped elsewhere are powerless compared to him (96:4–6; 97:7–9; 135:15–18). He sovereignly chose Israel as his special people (33:12; 95:6–7; 105:6; 135:4) and their king, particularly David (78:70; 89:3–4), as his representative.

The psalms are concerned about the nature of his rule. Power corrupts and many rulers oppress. But God reigns in righteousness and holiness, administering a true justice in his court (47:8; 93:5; 96:13; 97:2, 6, 8; 98:9; 99:4). He especially looks out for those who suffer injustice at the hands of the powerful (10:16–18; 68:5–6; 82:1–8; 146:9–10).

The united witness of the Psalms is: 'The Lord Most High is awesome, the great King over all the earth' (47:2). He is worthy not only of praise, but also of receiving our submission and obedience too.

 ORIENTATION: This simple meditation, chiefly in the wisdom tradition, arises from a deep, godly conviction.

 MAP: Like Psalm 1, it revolves around a strong contrast.

The wickedness of the wicked, 1–4

They are described as:

- practical atheists, 1: 'no fear of God';
- blindly arrogant, 2: 'they flatter themselves';
- foolishly deceitful, 3: their words 'are wicked and deceitful';
- knowingly evil, 4: 'they commit themselves to a sinful course'.

The goodness of the Lord, 5–9

The psalmist, representing the righteous, celebrates:

- the immensity of God's love, 5–6b: 'the highest mountains . . . the great deep';
- the breadth of God's love, 6c: 'people and animals';
- the value of God's love, 7: 'priceless';
- the abundance of God's love, 8: 'feast' and 'river of delights';
- the benefits of God's love, 9: 'life . . . light'.

The meditation ends with a prayer of response, in vv. 10–12, for God's covenant love to continue and to provide protection for the righteous in the face of evil.

LINKS: The first part of this psalm is developed and expanded in Rom. 1:18–32.

SIGNPOST: 'Whatever happened to sin?' Contemporary society is characterized by a denial of sin and human responsibility for it. Wrong behaviour is explained (or excused) in psychological (genes or illness), social (poverty or lack of education) or even political terms ('it's the government's fault'), but not in moral and spiritual terms. Here, and frequently elsewhere in the Bible, the psalmist is not afraid to name wickedness for what it is and attribute its cause to an absence of the fear of God. He does not glory in wickedness and make too much of it – he soon passes on to the positive goodness of God – but he doesn't ignore it either. A sick person has no hope of a cure until what is wrong is correctly diagnosed. Should we be more honest about sin in society? In what ways can we help society identify the root cause of its problems?

Wicked men and loving God

Cool down

 ORIENTATION: This psalm addresses a very common problem: we get angry and perplexed because the wicked seem to do so well (vv. 1–2). Where is the God of justice in it all?

MAP: The psalm responds by inviting us to consider:

Spiritual principles, 3–7
Using a veritable thesaurus of words – 'trust . . . delight . . . commit . . . be still . . . wait' – it invites us to focus positively on God rather than negatively on the wicked.

Emotional practices 8, 16, 34
Among other advice, the psalmist invites us to:
- control anger, 8: it only makes matters worse;
- cultivate contentment, 16: 'better the little . . . than the wealth . . .'
- maintain hope, 34: 'in the Lord', not some impersonal fate;
- remain obedient, 34: 'and keep his way'.

Future prospects, 9–40
As in Psalm 73, the real answer lies in seeing the bigger picture. Taking the long-term perspective, we can see:
- the judgment of the wicked;
- the vindication of the righteous.

Note especially v. 11, which is reinforced by the teaching of Jesus in Matt. 5:5.

LINKS: This psalm has a companion one in Psalm 73.

SIGNPOST: 'What's the point?' Numerous believers have posed that question down the centuries as they have seen well-behaved, law-abiding God-fearers get the rough end of life, while those who are careless about spiritual matters, if not downright wicked, seem to swan their way through life and enjoy prosperity. It makes them ask whether being godly is worth it. Ecclesiastes explores this very problem: 'There is something else meaningless that occurs on earth: the righteous who get what the wicked deserve, and the wicked who get what the righteous deserve' (8:14). On the surface Ecclesiastes seems to suggest that it's just another illustration of the futility of life, so we might as well stop worrying about it and get on with enjoying life. But a careful reading of Ecclesiastes suggests some deeper answers. It's meaningless only if you don't take God and eternity into account. He has given life to be enjoyed, he watches over it still, and he 'will bring every deed into judgment' (12:14). Ecclesiastes is worth reading.

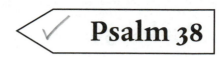

✓ **Psalm 38**

ORIENTATION: This is the third penitential psalm (see Ps. 6). The psalmist is struggling with severe illness, which he sees as God's judgment. He admits sin is his problem (vv. 5, 18). He cries out for relief from his distress.

MAP: Charting his low (if realistic) state of mind, the psalmist dwells on:

The discipline of the Lord, 1–8
He sees his condition as due to God's correction of his sin. It is:
- awfully severe, 1–3;
- thoroughly deserved, 4–5;
- physically crushing, 6–8.

The desertion of friends, 9–14
God's evident judgment on his life has social consequences:
- God is his only true companion, 9;
- others have proved failed companions, 10–12;
- his true state is one of loneliness, 13–14.

The discomfort of the heart, 15–22
He feels discomfort in every dimension of his life. There is:
- discomfort in waiting, 15–16;
- discomfort in body, 17;
- discomfort in confession, 18;
- discomfort with friends, 19–20;
- discomfort with God, 21–22. Will he come quickly?

Unusually, this psalm leaves the problem unresolved. God surely will forgive, but he doesn't do so before this psalm is complete. It teaches us to take confession seriously and avoid thinking a quick apology is all that's needed.

SIGNPOST: 'I must have been bad, or I wouldn't be ill like this.' How often I've heard this in my pastoral visits. It's a popular belief. The psalmist clearly believes his illness is a punishment from God. But Christians have tended recently to play down any direct connection between sin and suffering, just as Jesus seems to do in Luke 13:1–5 and John 9:1–5. Are we justified in doing so? Forgiving sin and healing the body are often interwoven in the Gospels. See Mark 2:1–12; John 5:1–15; 8:1–11. The Greek word *sozo* sometimes means 'saved' and sometimes 'healed'. And what about Paul's comment in 1 Cor. 11:27–31? May God not discipline us through sickness on occasions? Isn't there a connection between a God-centred life and a healthy one?

Psalm 39

 ORIENTATION: The old song 'This world is not my home, I'm just a-passing through . . .' sums up the central message of this psalm. The whole of life is brought into focus by an awareness of how short it is (see vv. 4–6, 12). Our residence on earth is not permanent.

MAP: A clear perspective is gained in three areas:

His frustrations are brought into focus, 1–3
The psalmist describes how he tries to cope with the enigma of life's brevity:
- he tries to discipline the tongue, 1–2a: to say nothing ill of God;
- but he succeeds only in building up frustrations, 2b–3: as he represses his feelings.

His finiteness is brought into focus, 4–6
Remembering how fragile and finite life is, the psalmist sees how futile it is to get worked up about things over which he ultimately has no control.

Faith is brought into focus, 7–13
The best response to the brevity of life is to live a life of faith:
- faith brings hope, not resignation, 7–8;
- faith brings relief through prayer, 9–11;
- faith brings joy through the struggles, 12–13.

LINKS: Eccl. 2:17–26 and 5:10–15 develop the same theme.

SIGNPOST: Within a few days of my mother's death at 83, Greg Parsons, a lovely 26-year-old student at our college, was killed in a road accident. The contrast between them was great. My mother lived a long life. Diagnosed with cancer 18 months before she died, she had time to get everything in order and take her leave of family and friends. She looked back with gratitude on the life God had given her. Greg died suddenly. He, and we, thought his life was ahead of him. Given the impact he'd already made, what a life it would have been. But it finished without warning. No time to sort things out or say goodbye. Verses 4–5 became very real to us as we grieved. Since we cannot know how long or short our lives will be, we should make the most of every day God gives.

 ORIENTATION: Unusually, this psalm starts on a high and ends on a low. Some think it is two psalms put together in the wrong order! But perhaps it is true to experience, since our spiritual lives are not always straightforward.

MAP: Here is:

A testimony of deliverance, 1–3

The psalmist looks back on the Lord rescuing him and the song it put into his life.

A reflection on deliverance, 4–10

As he reflects more widely on that deliverance, so he speaks of:

- the greatness of God's salvation, 4–5;
- the nature of God's demands, 6–8;
- the company of God's people, 9–10: this stresses the importance of testimony.

A longing for deliverance, 11–17

His joyful certainty gives way to agonizing uncertainty. Life has its ups and its downs. So he ends up expressing:

- an urgent cry to God, 11–15, which leads to
- a determined hold on God, 16–17: here the head seems to be instructing the heart.

LINKS: Verses 6–8 express hesitancy about endless sacrifices, recognizing that they can become a cheap substitute for the real offering God requires, that of obedient lives. Heb. 10:5–7 applies this to Christ. See note on 'The Psalms and the letter to the Hebrews' (p. 191).

SIGNPOST: Past victories are no guarantee of future success. The psalmist who begins by rejoicing in God's deliverance soon finds himself plunged into despair once more. His past gives him a grip on God, but even so his present troubles are so real that his ability to cope with them is limited. Life's like that. It's not always a smooth path from one victory to another. Some saints who've known the sunshine of God on their lives feel the darkness descend in old age and others who've served God well, such as Gideon (Judg. 8) and Joash (2 Chr. 24), begin well but do not last the course. What lessons of God's faithfulness see us through the troubles yet to come? Job 2:10 might help. What steps can we take to build a steady walk with God? What might Gal. 6:1 have to say to us?

True to experience

Zion and the temple

For us, the city of Jerusalem has become a city of controversy and conflict, and its temple is hardly even a memory. But attention is frequently drawn to the hill of Zion (on which Jerusalem is located), the city of Jerusalem and the beauty of the temple in the Psalms (e.g. 11, 46, 48, 68, 76, 84, 87, 122 and 137). They are viewed with pride and affection. Their existence is a cause of thanksgiving and their protection is sought. It sounds nationalistic and territorial. Why is such attention paid to them?

Their significance lies in what they represent. God is to be found there. Although God reigns in heaven, the temple in Jerusalem is his dwelling place on earth (11:4; 43:4; 46:4–6; 68:16; 132:13–14). It is there people come to find him and worship him with songs, sacrifices, testimonies and vows (22:22–31; 27:4; 40:9–11; 48:9; 50:1–3, 14; 66:13).

From there God rules on earth through his chosen king (2:6–9). The emphasis on the king being installed in 'Zion, my holy mountain' stresses the religious and moral nature of his rule, not just its political aspect. This is emphasized too in God's refusal to permit David as a 'man of blood' to build the temple (2 Sam. 7) and in the stress laid on those who go to worship being expected to live 'blameless' lives (15, 24).

The hill, the city and the temple are tangible symbols of the faithfulness of God in keeping his promise to provide Israel with a land and David with a place for his throne. Psalm 68 marks a significant stage in that process, even though the temple is still to be built, as it celebrates the entry of the ark of the covenant into Jerusalem. See 2 Sam. 6. But these psalms are not nationalistic and, with the prophets Isaiah and Ezekiel, look forward to the day when people of all nations will come to worship there and live in the light of the Lord (47, 87).

Christians no longer have a geographical centre to our faith. Our centre is the risen Christ (Acts 7:44–53). The old Jerusalem merely foreshadowed 'the city of the living God, the heavenly Jerusalem' (Heb. 12:22) to which we belong.

Psalm 41

ORIENTATION: Much of Book 1, which this psalm concludes, has been concerned with David as king. It was the particular responsibility of the king to have mercy on the weak. As with the other books, this one concludes with a doxology (v. 13).

 MAP: There is a three-part consideration of mercy here:

Mercy is commended, 1–3

Practising mercy towards the weak leads to:

- a happy life;
- the Lord's protection.

Mercy is requested, 4–9

The king who should exercise mercy now requests mercy for himself in view of:

- the discipline of the Lord, 4;
- the defamation of his enemies, 5–6;
- the disease of the body, 7–8: was he really suffering, or was it just a slur?
- the desertion of friends, (see John 13:18).

Mercy is experienced, 10–13

God's mercy upholds and delivers him. Verse 10b strikes a jarring note – one about which Matt. 18:21–35 might have something to say.

LINKS: See Prov. 31:1–9 (esp. vv. 8–9) for the responsibility of kings towards the weak. This psalm is a commentary on Jesus' saying, 'Blessed are the merciful, for they will be shown mercy' (Matt. 5:7).

SIGNPOST: The call for God's people to exercise mercy is a frequent message in the prophets. To show mercy is to show practical compassion towards an offender or one who is weak or powerless. Key verses are found in Hos. 6:6, 'For I desire mercy, not sacrifice'; Mic. 6:8, 'What does the Lord require of you? To act justly and to love mercy'; Mic. 7:18, 'Who is a God like you, who . . . delight[s] to show mercy'; and Zech. 7:9, 'This is what the Lord Almighty said: "Administer true justice; show mercy and compassion to one another."' Other prophets, such as Amos, emphasize the need for mercy in different words, but perhaps the most extended treatment of it is found in Isa. 58. Read it and see how much mercy weighs on God's heart, how wrong it is to substitute religious observance for the exercise of practical mercy, and what blessing living a merciful life brings in its wake. Is there a practical act of mercy you can do today?

Blessed are the merciful

Psalm 42 ✓

ORIENTATION: Book 2 starts on a down note. 'Why . . . are you downcast?' (v. 5). This psalm betrays all the hallmarks of spiritual depression with some clues about how to escape it.

MAP: The psalm offers an elementary guide to spiritual depression.

The character of depression, 1–4

The psalmist is geographically a long way from the temple, but his sense of distance from God is just as real and is manifest in:

- an unsatisfied longing for God, 1–2;
- an uncontrolled flow of tears, 3a;
- an unanswerable barrage of taunts, 3b (and 10);
- an uninhibited sighing for the past, 4.

The causes of depression, 5

As so often in facing any illness, the questions arises, 'Why?' Depression may have any number of causes of an internal or external kind. Here no clear answer is given, but there are a number of hints about its cause, including: opposition (3), isolation (4), separation from home (6), and pressure (7) which seems overwhelming. Mount Hermon, the source of the River Jordan, was as far away from Jerusalem as you could get in Israel.

The cure for depression, 5b–11

Though not the complete answer, the psalmist sets out some initial steps worth following:

- talk to yourself, speaking sense, 5b, 11;
- keep up the routines of spiritual discipline, 8;
- hold on to God even in the darkness, 9.

SIGNPOST: Depression is a very common illness and we need to treat those who suffer from it with care. It's foolish telling them to 'snap out of it'. We are complex creatures in which the physical, mental, emotional and spiritual aspects of our being all interact with each other. The cause of the depression may lie in another area, but will find expression in the emotions. Finding a cure usually requires a holistic approach. Spiritual depression can be as real as other forms of depression, but is often unrecognized. People who are depressed often need gentle support, space, a listening ear and *practical* help, particularly if the cause is isolation or stress. Do you know folk who are depressed? What can you do to lighten their burden?

ORIENTATION: This reads like a continuation of the previous psalm, with v. 5 repeating 42:5 and 11. Though the struggle with depression continues, the tone is slightly more positive, as though emotional strength is being regained.

MAP: Here petition alternates with affirmation.

First petition, 1
'Vindicate me . . . rescue me.'

First affirmation, 2
'You are God my stronghold.'
But this leads to the question of why God seems absent.

Second petition, 3
'Send me your light.'
The image of light is that of a torch shedding light on a path so the troubled person can find their way out of darkness and reach the secure destination of the temple.

Second affirmation, 4
'Then I will go . . . '
He commits himself to praise God again who is 'the source of all my joy' (NLT).

Soliloquy, 5
'Why, my soul, are you downcast?'
He challenges his low feelings and seeks to raise his level of faith.

SIGNPOST: This comment should be read in conjunction with the comment on Psalm 42. In his classic book *Spiritual Depression: Its Causes and Cure* (Pickering and Inglis, 1965), Martyn Lloyd-Jones wrote (pp. 20–21) of the paradoxical need to talk to oneself but not to listen to oneself. By listening to oneself he meant the times when the mind is in neutral and brings problems, accusations and thoughts of worthlessness to the fore. By talking to oneself he means doing exactly what Psalms 42 and 43 do. 'The main art in the matter of spiritual living is to know how to handle yourself. You have to take yourself in hand, you have to address yourself, preach to yourself, question yourself. You must say to your soul: "Why art thou cast down" – what business have you to be disquieted? . . . "Hope thou in God" . . . And then you must go on to remind yourself of God, who God is, and what God is and what God has done, and what God has pledged himself to do.'

Psalm 44 ✓ ⟩

ORIENTATION: This psalm is a national lament rather than an individual one, though the presence of the individual peeps through in v. 6. It is composed at a time when faith and facts do not stack up.

MAP: The psalm develops in four stages.

What we heard, 1–3

The nation's memory is full of:

- what God did, 2: he crushed the enemies;
- how God did it, 3: in an unconventional way.

Where we stand, 4–8

There is nothing wrong with their commitment to God. They protest their:

- faithfulness to God, 4;
- trust in God, 5–6;
- experience of God, 7;
- boasting about God, 8.

Why we're confused, 9–22

Verse 9 begins with a big 'But'. Why is God silent?

- they have failed in battle, 9–16;
- yet they are firm in faith, 17–22.

What we want, 23–26

- 'Wake up, Lord, and stop hiding yourself from us.'

LINKS: Verse 22 voices despair and seems like an accusation against God, in spite of their commitment to him. Rom. 8:36 uses it in a very different way and in an altogether positive context.

SIGNPOST: Aimee Semple McPherson was a controversial and somewhat eccentric evangelist who founded the Pentecostal Angelus Temple in the early twentieth century. In opening her crusade in San Jose in 1921, she preached on the subject, 'Is Jesus the great I am or the great I was?' The historical basis for our faith is crucial, as Israel knew. Yet to be trapped in history and only have a God who did things yesterday is a tragedy. Psalm 44 expresses just this anguish. Do we have any experience of God that is only about what 'we have heard with our ears' and what 'our ancestors told us', or can we testify to a God who is also powerfully at work in the present? Is he 'the same yesterday, today and for ever' (Heb. 13:8)?

 ORIENTATION: This was originally composed as a wedding song for the Davidic king.

 MAP: The wedding is considered from two angles:

The glories of the king, 1–9

His glories are seen in:

- the attractiveness of his person, 2, in character and physique;
- the success of his battles, 3–5, stresses his majesty;
- the stability of his throne, 6a;
- the justice of his reign, 6b–7;
- the magnetism of his influence, 8–9. He doesn't smell of the battlefield, but is blessed by precious spices, goods and women from all over the world.

The duties of the bride, 10–17

It is said she needs to:

- concentrate, 10b, on the king, not the past;
- reciprocate, 11, his delight in her;
- appreciate, 12, her position in the world;
- radiate, 13–14, for the sake of her husband;
- anticipate, 16, the future with confidence.

LINKS: Heb. 1:8–9 rightly applies this psalm to Jesus, the King of kings, who hailed from the line of David. George Whitefield used it to preach to young women on 'Christ, the best husband'.

SIGNPOST: Consider the two aspects of this psalm. First, take the qualities that are attributed here to the earthly king and apply them to the one who is 'the ruler of the kings of the earth' (Rev. 1:5). Use them as the basis for a prayer meditation on the glories of his kingship. Second, remember that the New Testament calls the church the bride of Christ in 2 Cor. 11:2; Eph. 5:22–23 and Rev. 21:2, 9. How does the contemporary church measure up in its fulfilment of the responsibilities of the bride as set out in Psalm 45:10–17? What constructive steps can we take not to condemn the church for her failures, but to encourage her in the fulfilment of her obligations to her bridegroom?

Exile and return

The lowest point in Israel's history came when they went into exile in Babylon. Successive deportations of the people took place from 597 BC onwards after many years of weakness. The story is told in 2 Kgs 24 – 25 and 2 Chr. 36, with the whole traumatic experience being reported in Jeremiah. It was Egypt all over again. Only this time they had only themselves to blame. Despite many warnings and the occasional attempt at reform, their increasing breaking of the covenant had brought them to feel the full weight of God's wrath. It was nothing more than the covenant had promised.

Several psalms give voice to the disorientation (to use Brueggemann's word) Israel felt when they watched Jerusalem destroyed and the temple razed to the ground, and found themselves turfed out of their homeland. Psalm 44 is an example of the defeated nation expressing its anguish. Since, however, most psalms are far from clear about their historical settings, it isn't always possible to be certain whether psalms are speaking of the exile or of other dark episodes in Israel's life. But Psalms 74 and 79 are usually judged to concern the exile, and were probably designed as prayers to use in the services Israel still held in captivity. In them they cry for God's help as they describe the humiliation they felt and pour out their bewilderment at or confession for causing the turn of events. The sense of rejection dominates these poems. Psalm 137 is the best-known and most poignant of such expressions with its haunting question, 'How can we sing the songs of the Lord while in a foreign land?'

Looking to the future, some psalms pray for their return (80, 85) or anticipate it keenly (107). They felt the very honour of God was at stake unless his people were restored (79:9–11). Psalm 12 exuberantly offers praise for their return and speaks of the laughter and joy they felt when the Lord restored their fortunes. The end of exile at the hand of the pagan king Cyrus (Isa. 45) was seen by them as the Lord's doing.

 ORIENTATION: 'God is our refuge and strength, an ever-present help in trouble.' These marvellous words, the first verse of this psalm, are usually quoted at the start of a funeral service and are always a truth people hang on to during days of difficulty, as they did in the last world war. And rightly so, for the psalm is all about discovering the power of God in the midst of chaos.

MAP: The psalm sketches the various quarters where chaos is found.

In the chaos of creation, 2–3
God is our refuge when the earth behaves unpredictably because of earthquakes or tsunamis.

In the chaos of the city, 4–7
When others may be plotting and working for the downfall of the city, God dwells within her and rules over all.

In the chaos of the conflict, 7–11
When the nations of the earth fight, he works peace. So, quieten your troubled hearts, for 'The Lord Almighty is with us; the God of Jacob is our fortress' (vv. 7, 11).

SIGNPOST: Verse 10 is often quoted at the start of a prayer meeting or to encourage people on a retreat to slow themselves down, disconnect from the concerns of their busy lives and focus on God. It is usually meant to conjure up the image of 'green pastures and quiet waters' from Psalm 23:2, but while that has its place, it is not really what Psalm 46 is about. The stillness we need to discover in knowing that God is the Lord Almighty comes in the midst of the chaos of battle, not when we withdraw from it. This is a verse not for the contemplative monk so much as for the harassed mother with restless young children, the busy executive with pressing decisions, the teacher in a classroom of uncontrollable teenagers, the factory-floor worker in a noisy assembly plant and the missionary in an alien religious culture where she is not welcomed. Can you pray this, and claim the promise of v. 1, for yourself, or for others facing chaos today?

Psalm 47 ✓

 ORIENTATION: This joyful psalm invites the crowd (v. 1) to celebrate God's reign over all the earth. It could have been a processional psalm sung at the enthronement of King David, but the wording of v. 2 reflects Sennacherib's arrogant claim about himself in Hezekiah's day (see Isa. 36) and so this psalm may be a response to him. Either way, it forces us to look to the future when everything will be subjected to God's rule (1 Cor. 15:20–28).

MAP: Here we rejoice that God is:

Awesome in his nature, 2
'The Lord Most High is awesome.'

Gracious in his election, 3–4
'He chose our inheritance' (see Deut. 7:7–9).

Universal in his reign, 5–9
'King of all the earth.'

Established on his throne, 8
'God is seated on his holy throne.'

Spurgeon wrote, 'In nature, in power, in character, in glory, there is none to compare with him. Oh, glorious vision of a coming era!'

SIGNPOST: The ascension of Jesus is one of the most neglected festivals in the Christian calendar, with many Christians not knowing quite what to make of it. Luke 24:50–53 and Acts 1:9 record the event, but, apart from being a way of removing Jesus from the earth, what does it mean? The cloud and the mountain recall God's appearance at Sinai (Exod. 19). God comes down to take Jesus up and, now that his mission on earth has been accomplished, enthrone him at the heart of our creation. Acts 2:33–36 spells this out. Jesus is now 'exalted to the right hand of God', has released his Spirit on earth and is confirmed as 'both Lord and Messiah'. Heb. 4:14–16 explains further that we have a sympathetic and 'great high priest' to represent us in God's throne room as a result. Rev. 5 pictures the scene and reminds us, in v. 6, that the lamb who is worshipped looks 'as if it had been slain'. The exalted Christ carries the wounds of his humanity with him, making him well qualified to represent us weak human beings to his Father.

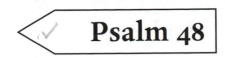

Psalm 48

 ORIENTATION: This psalm not only celebrates the magnificent features of Jerusalem but, more importantly, invites us to consider what it says about God. Verse 14 suggests that it teaches us 'what God is like'.

MAP: The qualities of the city celebrated here are:

Its magnificent character, 1–3
Its location matches its calling as the city of God, 'the Great King'.

Its astonishing impact, 4–7
A worldwide conspiracy to overthrow Jerusalem was defeated by the invading armies being overawed by its sheer magnificence. Although we cannot confidently identify such an incidence, this may refer to Isa. 37:36.

Its secure future, 8
Historical reflection now gives way to personal testimony that boldly affirms the city's future security.

Its central feature, 9–11
The focal point of the city is the temple and, hence, the presence of God within her.

Its spiritual significance, 12–14
Inspecting the city reminds you of all that God has done and that this is 'our God', the God of the covenant, who will guide his people into the future.

LINKS: 1 John 1:1–2 echoes v. 8 in the importance of seeing and hearing.

SIGNPOST: I shall never forget my first visit to Jerusalem. We had arrived in the dark, but when I opened the curtains early the next morning and looked across the valley to the city, it was magnificent. I could understand why the psalmist was moved to compose this song. But his real point is to recall that it is God's city. He chose it, as it were, as his address on earth and gave it, in a remarkable way, to his elect people. Whatever happened in the future, no-one could deny what they had heard and seen take place there (v. 8). When it is hard to believe, we look to concrete evidence to convince us that we are not mistaken. Jerusalem was one such piece of evidence for the children of Israel. What are the concrete markers in your life that you look to when doubt looms?

Psalm 49 ✓

ORIENTATION: The riddle that this wisdom psalm examines is one that applies to everyone, as vv. 1–4 state. The negative refrain found in vv. 12 and 20 ('Human beings . . . are like the beasts that perish') properly marks its main divisions.

MAP: The following analysis may prove more helpful than the formal structure.

The riddle announced, 1–4
And the audience summoned.

The riddle posed, 5–6
The question is: how is it possible to avoid being afraid when we face troubling times or troublesome people, who 'cushion themselves (against difficulty) by heaping up wealth' (VanGemeren)?

The riddle solved, 7–15
The psalmist dwells on two facts that solve the riddle for him. Concerning the rich:

- in life, they face a common death with the poor, 7–11;
- in death, they experience a contrasting fate to the poor, 12–15, without hope of redemption.

The riddle applied, 16–20
As a result:

- there is no need to be intimidated by the rich, 16–19;
- there is every need to gain understanding, 20.

'Sleep after toil, port after stormy seas, ease after war, death after life does greatly please' (Edmund Spenser, *The Faerie Queene*, 1, ix, 40).

SIGNPOST: It's rare to find hope of a meaningful life after death in the OT, but v. 15 provides a glimmer. It was usually thought that when a person died they were consigned to Sheol, a land of hollow existence but no real substance where people were estranged from God. See Psalm 88:10–12; 115:17. Later the Jews came to believe in a general resurrection at the end of time. But our understanding of the afterlife has been transformed by the resurrection of Christ. After death we now hope to enter into a fuller life, not a lesser one, unencumbered by the corrupting forces we presently face (1 Cor. 15:35–57), to be spent joyfully in God's presence (Phil. 1:21–23). The psalmists' desire will come to fruition. Our future hope should have a present impact. See 1 Cor. 15:58.

 ORIENTATION: God's people, which means all of them around the globe, not just Israel, are summoned into his courtroom to hear charges read out against his people.

MAP: The courtroom scene explains:

Who is the judge? 1–6
The psalm speaks of him as:

- the mighty God who is Creator, 1;
- the radiant God who is perfect, 2;
- the awesome God who is Judge, 3–6.

What are the charges? 7–21
There are two counts on the charge sheet, both of which relate to worship:

- Israel generally has demonstrated debased attitudes, 7–15, by assuming God is dependent on their sacrifices.
- The wicked specifically have demonstrated gross indifference, 16–21, by ignoring God's word in their actions.

What is the verdict? 14–15, 22–23
While all are undoubtedly guilty, the verdicts are surprisingly gracious:

- Israel is invited to renew her trust in God, 14–15.
- The wicked are invited to repent of their sin before God, 22–23.

SIGNPOST: Sadly, worship has proved a battleground in many churches today, with debates about singing and musical instruments distracting us from the real essence of worship. What would this psalm look like if written in a contemporary idiom? Would it go something like this? 'I cannot fault you for the number of songs you sing, but I have no need of them for the downloads on a thousand iPods are mine. Am I kept alive by your singing? And why do you endlessly mouth truths about me, but then forget them and live by a different code as soon as you've left the church?' Have a go at rewriting this psalm yourself to bring it up to date, so that it can regain something of its initial impact.

'The name of the Lord is to be praised'

'What is the chief end of man?' Answer: 'Man's chief end is to glorify God and enjoy him for ever.' These opening words of the Westminster Shorter Catechism could not describe praise in the Psalms more perfectly. Around a quarter of the psalms are hymns of praise to God; some declare it, some invite it, while others describe why he is worthy of it. Praise psalms are found throughout, but their frequency increases in the last two books (90 – 106 and 107 – 150). An illustration of this is seen in 103 – 107. The shortest psalm, 117, is a model hymn of praise.

Praise and God. God is not in need of praise, as if his ego requires boosting – but he longs to relate to his creation and his creatures need to approach him appropriately. When Psalm 22:3 says God is 'enthroned on the praises of Israel', it doesn't mean that he depends on Israel's worship to uphold his reign, but that Israel's praise 'surrounds' his throne (see NLT). He is worthy of praise as Creator, Saviour, Sovereign and Provider. The reasons for praising him stretch from before creation, through Israel's story of exodus, conquest, monarchy, exile and restoration, to the future yet to come, which is safe in his hands (48:14). As he is the supreme sovereign, even opposition to him is transformed into his praise (76:10). All creation is summoned to praise him (148), including Israel and the nations, people, creatures and nature. They are summoned to do so every day (113:3) and by every possible means (150).

Praise and us. The psalmist recognizes that we need to stir our souls from lethargy (103:1–2), for we easily forget 'his benefits'. Hence many hymns begin with the command to 'Praise the Lord' (29; 47; 98; 113). Praising God is a good thing for human beings to do (92:1) and leads to us experiencing gladness, depth and understanding about life (92:4–6). Through praising God we are also able to win victories against our enemies (149:6–9), because praise evokes our trust in the God who was on our side.

'Great is the Lord and most worthy of praise' (145:3).

 ORIENTATION: This classic confession of sin arises out of David's adultery with Bathsheba, recorded in 2 Sam. 11 – 12.

 MAP: The psalm recounts:

The problem of sin: David's request, 1–2

David approaches God, recognizing:

- what sin is: transgression, iniquity and sin;
- what God has: compassion;
- what he needs: the blotting out of wrong and cleansing.

The seriousness of sin: David's repentance, 3–6

David demonstrates that genuine repentance involves:

- the need to admit sin's presence, 3;
- the need to confront its seriousness, 4;
- the need to acknowledge its depth, 5–6: it is inbred from the beginning.

The answer to sin: David's restoration, 7–9

David asks God to:

- 'de-sin' him, 7, by cleansing him;
- restore him, 8, to joy again;
- pardon him, 9, through removing his sin.

The victory over sin: David's renewal, 10–14

As a result of God's forgiveness, he looks to:

- become a new person, 10–12;
- have a new testimony, 13–15;
- engage in a new mission, 16–19.

SIGNPOST: The newspaper headlines scream 'Confessions of . . .' and then glory in the misdeeds of public figures. They merely reflect a society that boasts about the issues of which they should be ashamed. See Rom. 1:21–32. David's genuine confession after his affair with Bathsheba was different. He casts himself completely on God and makes no attempt to excuse himself. He knows how deep sin goes and how long-standing it is. It's not a one-off. Rather, he is sinful by nature. Only God's forgiveness brings hope and confession makes grace flow and brings relief. How seriously do you take sin, as an offence against God? Are there specific sins that you have never confronted and confessed? Or do you need simply to approach God again as a sinner by nature, asking for his joy to be renewed?

Whatever happened to sin?

Psalm 52

 ORIENTATION: The background to this psalm is found in 1 Sam. 21 – 22. David is on the run and comes to Nob. But Doeg, an Edomite, betrays to Saul those who help David and executes them. The story is about Doeg's thuggery and deception and Saul's paranoia and cruelty. But David is far from blameless and is himself a deceiver (see 1 Sam. 21:2). So David is caught out by his own psalm. The psalm has much to say to us today when politicians are corrupt and celebrity culture rules.

MAP: The three parts of this psalm relate to:

Empty heroes, 1–4
- what they are, 1c: 'a disgrace in the eyes of God';
- what they do, 1–2: boast and practise deceit;
- what they speak, 2–3: lies and destruction;
- what they love, 3–4: evil and falsehood.

Everlasting ruin, 5–7
- their end, 5a: 'God will bring you down';
- their example, 6–7: the righteous will learn from them;
- their error, 7: they trusted foolishly in wealth.

Enduring love, 8–9
The righteous testify that in contrast they experience:
- a flourishing life, 8: picture of the olive tree;
- a faithful love, 8c–d: 'for ever and ever';
- a firm hope, 9: 'I will hope'.

SIGNPOST: Somewhere James Montgomery Boice tells of a man who bought a couple of take away hamburgers one night. When he opened the bag he found that the day's takings had been put in the bag by mistake. What was he to do? As an honest man, he returned to the shop and handed them back to a grateful manager. The manager wanted to take his picture and send his name to the press. This man was a hero! Suddenly the man went coy. He begged the manager to say nothing because, he eventually explained, the woman in his car wasn't his wife, but a prostitute. All heroes are tarnished; many are flawed. When David says of Doeg, 'You call yourself a hero, do you?' and then protests about his deception and intrigue, David would do well to look in a mirror – as we all would when accusing others.

Repetition of
Ps. 14.

ORIENTATION and LINKS: With a few minor changes in wording, this psalm is a repeat of Psalm 14, where the reader will find the *Map*.

The major difference comes in v. 5, which, unfortunately, is capable of being translated in several ways. It probably refers to a sudden panic that besets atheists who attack God's people. Sennacherib's experience, recorded in 2 Kgs 18:13 – 19:37, is often thought to be in mind.

However, some, like Wilcock, point out that the psalms on either side clearly relate to David's times and the setting is much more likely to be that of 1 Sam. 21 – 26. In 1 Sam. 25 we read about David, foolish Nabal and his diplomatic wife Abigail: 1 Sam. 25:25 says, 'Nabal. He is just like his name – his name means Fool, and folly goes with him.' If this is right, Psalm 53:1 is a play on words and the psalm as a whole a comment on that episode.

Either way, one important lesson to grasp is that this psalm, like so many others, does not reflect a theoretical piety, but a devotion forged by experiencing God in real-life incidents with all their ups and downs.

SIGNPOST: One afternoon I happened to call unplanned on a lady in my church. It was just one of those impulsive visits. She greeted me with the words, 'Thank God you've come. You've stopped me doing something very stupid.' Very upset, she calmed down over a cup of tea, but she never told me what was really going on, although it related to problems in her marriage. I thought of this as I read David's comment to Abigail in 1 Sam. 25:32, 33: 'Praise the Lord . . . who has sent you to meet me today! Thank God for your good sense! Bless you for keeping me from murdering the man' (NLT). Can you recall times when an interruption has saved you from doing something foolish? Did you see it as 'a lucky coincidence' or, like David, did you thank God for it as a sign of his providence? Have you been used by God like this? Did you give God the credit or take it for yourself?

Psalm 54 ✓▷

The name of the Lord

The name of the Lord

 ORIENTATION: The context continues to be that of David's years as an outlaw and particularly his betrayal by his own (1 Sam. 23:19–29; 26:1–4). The central motif of the psalm is 'the name of the Lord' (vv. 1, 6).

 MAP: Three names for God are mentioned, each of which highlights a different aspect of God's character.

Elohim (God), 1, 2, 4a
God is *the supreme deity* who:
- saves the persecuted;
- hears his petitioners;
- helps the weak.

Adonai (the Lord), 4b
God is *the superior Lord* who:
- sustains his servants.

Yahweh (Lord), 6
God is *the covenant God* who:
- revealed himself to Moses;
- delivers and restores his people;
- causing them to rejoice.

SIGNPOST: In the ancient world, names summed a person up and were thought to reflect their character. So it is with God. Here we have three of his names. The most frequent is the name *Yahweh*, derived from the verb 'to be'. Given to Moses in Exod. 3:14, it become Israel's special covenant name for God. Some names were composed by adding to the word *El*, meaning 'the deity', or to *Yahweh*. So in Gen. 14:18–22 he is *el elyon*, 'God Most High'. In Gen. 17:1 God reveals himself as *el-shaddai*, 'God Almighty'. In Gen. 21:33 he is *el olam*, 'the eternal God'. In the story of the offering of Isaac he becomes *yahweh yir'eh*, 'the Lord will provide' (Gen. 22:8). In Exod. 17:15–16 he is *yahweh nissi*, 'The Lord my banner', and in Jer. 23:6 and 33:16 he is *Yahweh sidqenu*, 'the Lord our righteousness'. Other names have been identified, such as 'the Lord our healer' or 'the Lord our peace'. Pray through the significance of at least one of the above names for God. Do you have a favourite name for God? If so, why is it your favourite?

ORIENTATION: Psalm 55 is a long cry of anguish that is wrenched from the depths of David's being, not just because of his enemies' attacks, but more particularly because these enemies are his friends (see vv. 13–14, 20–21). The setting is unknown, but it may relate to his son Absalom's rebellion (2 Sam. 15 – 19) or his friend Ahithophel's conspiracy (2 Sam. 15:31, 34).

MAP: After expressing anguish and appealing for justice (vv. 1–8), the psalm voices confidence in God (vv. 9–19). It returns to the problem (vv. 20–21) before reflecting on God again (vv. 22–23).

   The key to handling the situation is found in the simple summary of v. 22: 'Give your burdens to the Lord, and he will take care of you. He will not permit the godly to slip and fall' (NLT). This verse contains:

An invitation
'Give your burdens to the Lord . . . '

An expectation
' . . . and *he will* take care of you.' This demonstrates a faith in God that arises from the psalmist's previous experience of him.

An explanation
'He will not permit the godly to slip and fall.' As a God of justice, he will preserve the saints, if they trust in him, and bring the wicked to judgment.

   This psalm repeats the cry of Psalm 41:9 when David spoke of a close friend's treachery. Jesus quoted that psalm in John 13:18 as he forecast Judas's betrayal.

SIGNPOST: Most of us know people who have been let down badly by husbands who've walked out on them, by children who've broken off with their parents, or gossips who've spoken treacherously of those who were friends. The wounds can be deep and lasting. What have we done to support them? David should have had friends to support him, but they made the situation worse. Christ commands us to 'Carry each other's burdens' (Gal. 6:2). Carrying a burden means more than praying or gossiping about it. It means sharing it. It may involve listening, being there when needed, helping with the kids, the shopping or the house, speaking common sense, or being a bridge of reconciliation. Can you identify someone whose burden of betrayal you should be carrying today?

When friends fail

Give thanks to the Lord

To offer praise is to focus on who God is; to offer thanks is to focus on what God has done and the benefits he confers on his people. The Psalms provide hymns of thanksgiving for occasions that involve the whole community and those which relate to single individuals. A common theme is that they have experienced God's deliverance in the face of some threat to their lives. The dominant style adopted as Israel approached God was that of praise and thanksgiving (100:4).

Communal thanksgivings speak of awesome events for which thanks are due. Psalm 66:5 typically invites us to 'Come and see what God has done, his awesome deeds for humankind!' It then recalls the crossing of the Red Sea as one of those mighty deeds for which thanks are due. However, the psalms on either side (65, 67) cite successful harvests as the cause for gratitude. Psalm 107 provides a catalogue of reasons for Israel's thankfulness. Psalm 118 offers thanks because the Lord answered prayer, proved a refuge and was with them as they faced their enemies. Psalm 124 is 'highly disciplined and intentional' (Brueggemann) in its thanksgiving and expresses gratitude that God was on Israel's side when various forces threatened chaos and destruction.

Thanksgiving, however, is more often associated with an individual who, having faced a crisis, testifies that the Lord comes to the rescue. The cause of the crisis in Psalms 30, 31 and 116 is illness; in Psalms 18, 92 and 118 it is hostility; in Psalms 32 and 40 it is the psalmist's sin that is the source of the problem. Psalm 66 is perhaps the most comprehensive of all, speaking of both personal and national distress, of individual trouble (v. 14) and countrywide oppression (vv. 11–12). 'He answered me' is the repeated cause of thanksgiving: a thanksgiving publicly acknowledged in the temple, or even more widely, and not kept for private celebration, and a thanksgiving that is used to inspire others to worship God (see 18; 30; 32; 66; 92; 116).

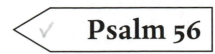

ORIENTATION: Still arising from David's fugitive years, this psalm shows the true stance of the believer when fear strikes. His first and only recourse is to God.

MAP: Various aspects of the relationship with God are outlined:

Mercy from God, 1–2, is sought. No rights are demanded – all that is asked for is mercy.

Trust in God, 3–4, is voiced. Where else could David go? God is superior to his enemies.

Avenged by God, 5–7, is his desire. God, not David, is to work justice and cause their wickedness to rebound on them. See Rom. 12:19.

Sustained by God, 8–11, through it all. God records his misery and is on his side. See Rom. 8:31–39.

Walking before God, 12–13, is the result. The outworking of his vow to God is that he enjoys a close companionship with God, walking in his 'life-giving light' (NLT).

SIGNPOST: When giving his testimony, the explorer and mountain-eer Bear Grylls described once suddenly falling a thousand feet into a crevasse and cartwheeling over and over. The ice pounding on him from above briefly knocked him out and when he came round he found himself 'gently penduluming' on the end of his rope. Panicking, he tried to clutch the walls and prayed the rope wouldn't break. It didn't. It was only a second or two before he fell that he'd clipped the rope on, but that rope saved his life. During his fugitive years David must have felt as if he had fallen into a crevasse. The rope that saved him in such extreme circumstances, according to vv. 4 and 10, was God's word. When human words failed him, God's word never did. It is, as Hebrews was to put it centuries later, 'an anchor for the soul, firm and secure'. Consequently, Hebrews tells us, whatever we face we may face it with hope and courage.

Psalm 57 ✓

 ORIENTATION: According to its title, 1 Sam. 22 – 27 gives the background of this psalm. David's fugitive years were times of extreme distress when the normal systems of support were removed. Verses 4 and 6 express his severe anguish while vv. 5 and 11 serve as a worshipful refrain.

MAP: The psalm speaks predominantly of God.

The protection of God, 1
God acts as a refuge whose wings shelter him.

The providence of God, 2
In spite of his circumstances, God will vindicate him, or, as in NLT, 'will fulfil his purpose' for him.

The promise of God, 3
He is confident that God will rescue him because of his covenant love. Motyer points out that the 'I cry out' of v. 2 is matched by the 'He sends' of v. 3.

The power of God, 5
His God is 'above the heavens . . . [and] over all the earth'.

The praise of God, 5, 7–11
David prays for God's glory (5, 11), affirms his faith (7), awakens his spirit (8), anticipates his future (9) and states that the reason for his praise is found in the greatness of God's love and the trustworthiness of God's character (10).

LINKS: Psalm 142 parallels this psalm.

SIGNPOST: Alec Motyer writes of David settling down to go to sleep in his cave at night and suddenly having an abrupt mood change as he grasps the truth about God. He writes, 'Nothing has changed, but everything is different. Prayer has become praise; the shadows (v. 1) have become the light of a new day (v. 8); the roar of lions (v. 4) has become the sweet sound of harp and lyre (v. 8). Prayer changes things; the Lord God changes things. *Tell him about it* (vv. 1–4); be assured that the emissaries of grace are on their way (v. 3); there is a moral destiny at work in the very nature of things which guarantees the downfall of evil (v. 6b). *So be resolute (v. 7); stick it out; wait for the dawn.*'

 ORIENTATION: One of the psalms that call for vengeance, this one reveals a 'passion for justice' (Kidner).

 MAP: It unfolds through four movements:

Contempt, 1–2
Nicely captured by NLT: 'Justice – do you rulers know the meaning of the word? . . . No, all your dealings are crooked.'

Contention, 3–5
The reason the rulers are evil is that:
- wickedness is inbred from birth, 3;
- and is aggravated by deafness to God, 4–5, as illustrated by the analogy of the snake and its charmer.

Condemnation, 6–9
The psalmist pours out a sevenfold litany, calling on God to condemn them by: (i) breaking their teeth, (ii) removing their fangs, (iii) making them disappear like water, (iv) making them fail in battle, (v) dissolving them like slugs, (vi) making them become like a stillborn child, and (vii) allowing them to be swept away like thorns.

Consequences, 10–11
The result of God's action will be that:
- the righteous are vindicated;
- the God of justice is revealed. Compare Rev. 14:20.

Note the language of v. 11 echoes that of v. 1 (ruler/God, speak/say, judge/judges, people/the earth) and provides an answer to the complaint expressed there.

LINKS: The vengeance psalms are 35, 59, 69, 70, 83, 109, 137 and 140.

SIGNPOST: Ouch! The 'gentle Jesus meek and mild' school of Christianity would find it impossible to ask God for vengeance as David does. We've learned to leave our real feelings outside and suspend angry passions, replacing them with warm thoughts and positive emotions during worship. Anger is always dangerous, since it can easily lead us into sin. But is it always wrong? Wasn't Jesus angry (Mark 11:12–21; John 11:33)? Eph. 4:26 teaches: 'In your anger do not sin: Do not let the sun go down while you are still angry.' Is there a clue here? Anger may be legitimate when directed at evil or an inevitable passion within us. But we're not to foster it or let it fester. Nor should we suppress it. We are to deal with it by forgiving the offender (Mark 11:25; Eph. 4:32) and giving it over to God (Rom. 12:17–21).

Psalm 59 ✓

ORIENTATION: 1 Sam. 19 tells the story behind this psalm, but it could apply to many occasions when his enemies surrounded David. In such circumstances, prayer always proves an effective counter-offensive (Phil. 4:6–7).

MAP: The shape of the psalm shows how carefully it was composed.

Stanza 1: Rescue me, 1–5
- from vicious suffering;
- from unjust suffering.

Chorus: From dogs to God, 6–10a
There are three subjects here – they (the enemies), you (God), and I (David):
- 'they' lack restraint;
- 'you' hold them up to ridicule;
- 'I' keep my eyes on God.

Stanza 2: Punish them, 10b–13
David requests:
- protection for himself;
- punishment for his enemies.

Chorus: From dogs to God, 14–17
- 'they': the enemies return;
- yet 'I': the psalmist rejoices;
- because of 'you': God is a refuge.

SIGNPOST: David twice refers to his enemies as 'snarling like dogs' who prowl the city at night (vv. 6, 14). It is an image that had already been used in Psalm 22:16, 20. Israelites did not think of dogs as tame and lovable pets. They were essentially viewed as wild, unclean animals with disgusting habits that roamed the streets in packs. They were vicious and dangerous, and being surrounded by them could be terrifying. David is, of course, speaking figuratively rather than literally. This means we can reapply the image, as we can other images in the Psalms. Who are the dogs in your life? What terrors strike you? It may be something from the past, either that you did and feel guilty about, or something done to you that you feel trapped by. It may be something from the present that threatens to overwhelm you and knock you off balance. Or it may be a fear of something that lies ahead and is yet to be experienced, but that too can paralyse. Does David's psalm help you to face the 'snarling dogs' in your life? Can 'you' place 'them' into the wider picture of 'him', the God who is a refuge?

ORIENTATION: The title locates this psalm in 2 Sam. 8 and 1 Chr. 18, which is puzzling since they record David's great victories. But there is more than meets the eye to the story. David's concentration in the north led to hostile neighbours invading his territory in the south. This psalm was composed in the face of that, with vv. 1 and 2 using the language of invasion.

MAP: Verse 4 could be taken in several ways, but the main outline is clear.

Rejected, 1–3

The reality of rejection is graphically described by:

- flood imagery, 1: 'burst upon us';
- earthquake imagery, 2: 'shaken the land';
- hangover imagery, 3: 'stagger'.

Resolved, 4–5

David turns to God in prayer for an answer:

- faith is affirmed, 4;
- deliverance is requested, 5.

Rescued, 6–8

The key to David's deliverance does not lie in his strength or strategy, but in what God decrees.

Restored, 9–12

David is restored to his throne:

- not by the help of human hands, 11;
- but by the help of God who gives us 'aid', 11.

SIGNPOST: 'Moab is my washbasin' (v. 8) sounds like the stuff of a spoof sermon and was an ideal choice for Stephen Fry's initial autobiography. But to David, it and its neighbouring places were not a send-up. They deal in the realities of international politics and divine power. Shechem and Sukkoth (v. 6) were places God had given to David. Gilead, Manasseh, Ephraim and Judah (v. 7) recall the tribes settling under Joshua and David mentions their continuing value. Moab, Edom to the east, and Philistia to the west (v. 8) were neighbouring countries that were constantly hostile. But, however real their threat, David says they are nothing compared with his God. Moab is as unimportant as a washing-up bowl. Edom is as insignificant as a pile of shoes (the phrase probably hints at Edom's slave status). As sovereign of all, God decides the history of nations, and that's no spoof! Is your God a God who presides over international affairs or simply over individual lives?

Affirmations of faith

While it is clear that some psalms are composed as a result of a specific need, others seem to be more general compositions that affirm the psalmists' faith more generally. Psalm 23 might be the best-known one in this group. Other examples are found in 11, 16, 27, 46, 62, 63, 90, 91, 121, 131 and 148.

Affirmations of faith in the Psalms are more personal than the creeds said in most churches, even though those creeds begin 'I believe . . . ', and are certainly more personal than the 'statements of faith' many Christian organizations have which succinctly set out their doctrinal priorities. The psalmist is not saying 'I believe in my head', but 'I trust with my life'. They are critical statements of where the psalmists take their stand. The well-known opening words of Psalms 23, 46 and 90 illustrate the point. 'The Lord is *my* Shepherd, *I* lack nothing.' 'God is *our* refuge and strength . . . Therefore *we* will not fear . . . ' 'Lord, you have been *our* dwelling place throughout all generations.'

These psalms are not without statements that set out a rich doctrine of God. Look, for example, at the claims of Psalm 145, where we read that the Lord is great (v. 5), gracious (v. 8), compassionate (v. 8), good to all (v. 9), enduring (v. 13), trustworthy (v. 13), supportive of the weak (v. 14), generous (v. 15), righteous (v. 17), near to those who call (v. 18) and watching (v. 20). But it is clear from the opening and closing verses, as well as from the general tenor of the poem, that these statements are made much more as personal testimony than as abstract theological propositions.

The affirmations of the psalmists are based on the 'facts' of Israel's experience. They arise from how God has made himself known and what God has done in their history, but are never coldly objective statements. They are always warm and heartfelt statements of personal trust that grow out of a personal and covenant relationship. They blend truth with love and affection to perfection.

 ORIENTATION: It is difficult to place this lament in any original context. Verses 6–7, David's prayer for the king, could be a prayer for Saul. We know he sought to respect Saul as God's anointed king (see 1 Sam. 24:6; 26:9–11) even while on the run. Or it could be a prayer for himself, or a prayer voiced by a choir in response to his lament. No matter, for 'any child of God may pray this prayer for himself and for his messianic King' (VanGemeren).

MAP: The psalm expresses:

The distance felt, 1–2b
- a literal distance?, 2: 'from the ends of the earth';
- an emotional distance, 2: 'my heart grows faint'.

The protection sought, 2c–3
The rock is a very common and evocative image. Is it a reference to God, as so often, or is it a hankering after Jerusalem?

The nearness desired, 4–5
- a nearness to the God who is a refuge;
- which is his rightful place, given his heritage.

The blessing sought, 6–7
- a lengthy and godly reign.

The confidence expressed, 8
- the one who now laments will sing the praise of God again one day.

SIGNPOST: I read this psalm just after arriving at a refugee camp in northern Thailand. Everything was strange – indeed, the mirror opposite of what we were used to. There was much poverty, little food, no supermarkets, only patchy communications with the outside world, and no freedom. It seemed like 'the end of the earth'. So v. 2 had a special impact. God isn't confined to London, or to the Western world. He was as near and as ready to answer prayer on the other side of the world as he was at home. David was nowhere near as far from Jerusalem as we were from home, but the psalm speaks about the distance of the heart as much as the distance in miles. Our Karen refugee friends came from just over the hill in Burma, but felt so far from home. Wherever you are geographically or emotionally today, know with David, and the Karen, that you can call on the Lord.

The rock that is higher

Psalm 62 ✓ ⟩

ORIENTATION: Verses 3–4 make plain that David is feeling very vulnerable. His answer is to pour out his heart to God and find rest in him. The psalm causes us to question where we turn to find rest when we are stressed.

MAP: There are four key themes.

Trusting the Lord, 1–2, 5–7

David:

- finds security through God, 2: 'my fortress';
- practises silence before God, 5: 'find rest';
- discovers stability in God, 6: 'rock';
- receives salvation from God, 7: 'salvation'.

Facing the enemy, 3–4

- they are numerous;
- they are arrogant;
- they are deceptive.

Finding the way, 8–10

- try prayer, 8: 'pour out your hearts to him';
- gain perspective, 9, by bringing people down to size;
- review priorities, 10, and reject false ones.

Hearing the Lord, 11–12

Refreshment comes from:

- the clarity of God's word, 11;
- the character of God's person, 11–12: power and love.

SIGNPOST: There are times when I have felt like a 'tottering fence' (v. 3). The pressures of work have been so great that one more demand, one more request, one more push and, like a storm-battered fence only loosely secured in the ground, I would have collapsed. One of the ways I sought to avoid that in ministry was to take a quarterly retreat. One beautiful morning, on a prayer day with my colleagues, we read this psalm overlooking a wonderful view and began to 'find rest'. The psalmist reminds us that our rest doesn't come from pleasant scenery, or other common forms of escapism (though they have their place), but from God. It is by trusting him with our lives and pouring out our hearts to him (v. 8) that we find true stability and can cope with pressures. Look at the many ways this psalm speaks of him. No wonder he is able to strengthen us so that we do not totter over when the pressures come.

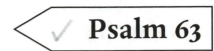
 ORIENTATION: Estate agents talk of location, location, location! What strikes me about this psalm is its sense of location. David's confession, 'You, God, are my God' (v. 1), speaks of a God who is adequate for every situation and never absent whatever one feels.

MAP: Several locations are mentioned.

God is sought in the desert, 1

David's sense of loneliness and thirst for God is evident as he is on the run. This refers either to 1 Sam. 23 or 2 Sam. 15.

God is seen in the temple, 2–5

In words that are reminiscent of Psalm 42, David recalls how good and glorious God was when he used to join in the great celebrations and festivals in the temple. Yet he has not changed and is the same God still.

God is scrutinized in the bedroom, 6–8

During the long, lonely hours of sleepless nights, David holds on to God as his only hope.

God is sensed in the battle, 9–11

Neither the memories of the temple nor the meditation of the night are escapist. Rather, they renew David's confidence in God and assure him that he will gain the victory over his enemies.

SIGNPOST: From the 1960s to the 1980s David Watson was one of Britain's most effective evangelists. He died from cancer in his early fifties. He told his story of coming to terms with cancer and squaring his suffering with the gospel he had preached in a couple of moving and honest books. In *Fear No Evil* (Hodder, 1984) he echoed David's experience in v. 8. 'Fears often loom large at night-time, when every negative thought can grow hideously out of proportion; but the daylight casts away the shadows and restores a right perspective.' In those long night hours the psalms proved a great comfort to David Watson: 'As I read and prayed through the psalms, I was conscious of my tensions unwinding, my fears disappearing and once again I was aware of the Lord's love surrounding me. I could literally rest in him.'

A God for everywhere

Psalm 64 ✓

A battle of arrows

 ORIENTATION: The threat faced in this individual lament is as real as it is unjust. Only God can deliver.

Parallelism in reverse order eg live to eat, not eat to live

MAP: The chiastic structure concerns God (vv. 1, 10); hidden conspiracy *v.* open plans (vv. 2, 9); wagging tongues (vv. 3, 8); their arrows *v.* God's arrows (vv. 4, 7) and cunning, wicked hearts (vv. 5, 6). But note the reference to arrows:

The arrows of the enemy 2–6
Their weapons consist of:

- secret conspiracies, 2;
- defamatory words, 3;
- brazen attitudes, 4;
- deluded minds, 5: 'Who will see it?'
- corrupt hearts, 6.

The arrows of the Lord, 7–10
By contrast David notes the following about the Lord's arrows:

- their finality, 7: 'suddenly . . . struck down';
- their justice, 8: Kidner entitles this psalm 'Measure for measure';
- their effect, 9: 'all people will fear';
- their righteousness, 10: right will triumph.

SIGNPOST: The psalmist seems to have a clear idea of who falls into the category of 'the wicked', as we often do. But v. 6 makes the more general statement that 'surely the mind and heart of man are cunning'. This suggests that we are *all* caught in the same net and are all capable of such wickedness. Our wickedness may not involve huge schemes to bring others down, but those tiny acts of deception in which we engage reveal the true state of our hearts. Jeremiah more confidently asserted that we are all tarnished with the same brush and even that the heart is capable of self-deception. 'The heart is deceitful above all things and beyond cure. Who can understand it?' (Jer. 17:9) Paul spoke in the same way in Rom. 7:15–20. But the Lord who searches the heart (Jer. 17:10) is also the Lord who can cure it. When did you last search your heart and face up to the darkness within? That's the first step to finding the cure.

ORIENTATION: This song of thanksgiving is remarkable for its blending of the personal and the global, the intimate and the awesome. It addresses God directly in the second person with a great sense of affection, rather than making statements about him in the third person.

MAP: This psalm speaks of a God of grace, greatness and goodness. He is:

A personal God who grants pardon, 1–4
There are three reasons why 'praise awaits you'. They are that:
- sins are forgiven, 3;
- access is provided, 4a: 'bring near';
- goodness is experienced, 4b.

A global God who creates peace, 5–8
This God:
- provides universal hope, 5;
- exercises universal power, 6–7;
- inspires universal praise, 8.

A generous God who provides plenty, 9–13
As they celebrate harvest they acknowledge God's provision as:
- abundant: 'abundantly . . . filled . . . bounty';
- reliable: 'crown the year' (see Gen. 8:22);
- evocative, as creation itself responds with shouts of praise.

SIGNPOST: Years ago, J. B. Phillips, who was well known at the time for translating the New Testament into modern English (still a great paraphrase), wrote a book called *Your God Is Too Small*. The title stuck with many. Psalm 65 throws up the question of how big our God is. It reveals a God who is both personal in his love and global in his rule. It also reveals a God who is about forgiving sin, ruling nations and providing food. He is not just a God of the spiritual, or even a God of the material, but a God of the political as well. He is the God of the small detail and of the international debate. He is one God, over all. Some churches I visit are wonderfully intimate fellowships that pray intensely for the needs of their members (often very small needs), but ignore the rest of the world. Some pray for the world, but ignore the needy persons in their pews. Some concentrate on the spiritual and some on the material. How far does our worship reflect the comprehensive God of Psalm 65?

'Trust in the Lord'

The theme of trust runs throughout the Psalms in the way the name of a seaside resort used to run though a stick of rock. Trust in God is seen as the default position of those who know him (9:10; 22:4), but needs to be actively maintained. It occurs in a number of different contexts.

First, it occurs as a statement of intent. The psalmist who is in dire trouble affirms that despite his circumstances he is going to trust the Lord. Psalms 13:5; 31:14; 52:8; 56:3, 4, 11 and 91:2 are examples of this. In this regard, it is no mere pious statement but often an expression of trust as the only hope the psalmist has in the situation he faces. If trust in God fails, he has no other option and his life is in danger. But he knows it won't.

Second, it occurs as an invitation. Israel's trust was often depleted and not as active or firm as it should have been, or deflected from God. Consequently, they failed to look to God when they should have done so and needed their faith to be stirred into flame again. Hence we read of frequent commands that Israel should trust in the Lord, as in 37:3; 62:8 and 115:9, 10, 11.

Third, the Psalms speak, in principle, of the value of trusting in the Lord. Trust in God brings joy (33:21), rewards (37:6) and blessing (40:4), banishes fear (56:4, 11) and provides stability (125:1).

Fourth, the Psalms warn against putting one's trust in things that will fail, whether it be princes, conventional weapons and armies (20:7; 44:6; 118:9; 146:3) or wealth and false idols (31:6; 49:6, 12–13; 135:15–18).

I once had a fascinating conversation with a Danish pole-vaulting champion. I couldn't conceive why anyone would thunder down a track and thrust themselves into the air, putting their whole weight on a slender pole as it catapulted them over a bar high above them. There is no better illustration of what the Bible means by trust. It is to stake one's life on, to put one's whole weight on, to rely exclusively on the Lord, as the pole-vaulter relies on the pole. If that lets you down, there is nothing that can come to the rescue. But while the pole occasionally snaps, the Lord will never fail.

ORIENTATION: God's people celebrate their deliverance from suffering even though God himself permitted it and then brought them through it (vv. 10–12). The psalm looks back to Egypt and the exodus.

MAP: It moves from 'communal affirmation to individual appreciation' of God (Brueggemann).

The people of God, 1–4
- What? They are invited to sing and shout, 1–2.
- Why? Because God's deeds are awesome, 3.
- Who? The people are not confined to Israel, but include 'all the earth', 4.

The power of God, 5–7
- Its people focus, 5: 'what awesome miracles he does for his people' (NLT).
- Its past evidence, 6, as in the exodus.
- Its permanent quality, 7: 'He rules for ever'.

The providence of God, 8–12
- Prevents us from stumbling, 9.
- Purifies us through suffering, 10–11.
- Provides us with salvation, 12, with ultimate grace.

The praise of God, 13–20
In expressing praise after suffering, the psalmist is:
- true to his word, 13–15;
- ready with his testimony, 16–20;
- aware of his need, 18, for holiness;
- settled in his heart, 20: 'not rejected'.

SIGNPOST: Suffering is never enjoyable, but it may serve the deeper purposes of God in our lives. Though the suffering spoken of here was severe (v. 11), God's people didn't reject him (v. 10), but saw it as his way of testing and refining them. Refining necessarily involves heating a metal until it turns to liquid so that all its impurities can be removed, leaving it pure and strong. Mal. 3:2–4 develops the same image. It recognizes the gravity of God acting like this, yet curiously says, 'He will sit as a refiner and purifier of silver . . .' Sitting down on the job doesn't suggest indifference to our suffering. Rather, it suggests his patience until the task is complete and his determination to ensure that all impurities are removed from our lives. His priority is our holiness, not our comfort. See Phil. 1:6, 10; Eph. 5:27 and 2 Pet. 3:14.

How awesome are your deeds

May God be gracious to us

 ORIENTATION: The repetition of 'peoples' and 'nations' means this psalm celebrates God as a universal God. Yet it begins with a prayer, patterned on Num. 6:24–26, for this same God to be gracious to Israel. The prayer, however, is not one for selfish comfort, but shows an awareness that election is always for service: 'that your ways may be known on earth' (v. 2).

MAP: Three of the 'ways' God does things are mentioned.

The 'way' of God's salvation, 2
Salvation, in v. 2b, flows from the grace mentioned in v. 1a.

The 'way' of God's sovereignty, 3–5
His rule is:

- global, 3: '*all* the peoples';
- just, 4b: contrary to many human rulers;
- wise, 4c: he guides in the paths of wisdom.

The 'way' of God's supply, 6–7
God shows his care in the ordinary by providing an abundance at harvest.

He saves, he rules, he provides. His 'ways' are not something to begrudge or endure, but to celebrate with joy.

SIGNPOST: The biblical idea of election was never a self-serving one. God did not chose Israel (Deut. 7:7) so that they could brag about their special status, but so that they could be the conduit of his blessing to the wider world. This was stated explicitly when he called Abraham. 'I will bless you . . . and you will be a blessing . . . all peoples on earth will be blessed through you' (Gen. 12:2–3). We are still saved to serve, elected to bless the nations. Let's examine ourselves to see whether that is how we are 'using' our salvation. How is God using us to bring the good news of his righteous reign to those of other nations? What part are we playing in world mission? If we're not, let's make a start today by getting informed, praying and supporting (yes, financially) those who are, even if we can't go and bring direct blessing to others overseas immediately. We've no right to keep God's rich blessing on our lives to ourselves.

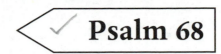

Psalm 68

 ORIENTATION: Composed for a festival procession (v. 24), this psalm is often associated with the return of the ark to Jerusalem (2 Sam. 6).

MAP: It interweaves the themes of majesty (God as the divine Warrior) and meekness (God as the compassionate Saviour).

Majesty

The dominant note is the strong one, stressing the majesty of God. The first line sets the tone: 'May God arise, may his enemies be scattered.' Strong imagery recalls the exodus and Sinai (7–8); the Promised Land (9–10); defeat of enemies (11–14); the holy city, Jerusalem (15–18 [compare 18 with Eph. 4:8]); judgment on the wicked (21–23); and God's power over creation (28–30). It is a call for God to rouse himself and use his awesome strength on behalf of his people.

Meekness

Yet there is a strong undercurrent of meekness, which qualifies the way in which God uses his power. So:

- he cares for the powerless, 5–6;
- he bears our burdens, 19, every day (unlike idols, who *are* burdens);
- he rescues from danger, 20, even death;
- he delights in his people, 24–27, from the less important ('young women') and the weak ('little tribe of Benjamin') to the very important ('princes');
- he strengthens his people, 35.

LINKS: For more on the ark of the covenant, see Exod. 25:10–22.

SIGNPOST: The tension between the meekness and the majesty of God is resolved at the cross of Christ. To all outward appearances, the cross spoke of Jesus going to his death meekly, like a lamb to the slaughter. As he went, his meekness was seen in his care of the powerless. Uncomplainingly, he was bearing our burdens (1 Pet. 2:24) and mysteriously rescuing us from our enemies (Col. 2:14–15; Heb. 2:14–15) by submission to a humiliating death: both aspects of God's characteristic meekness, according to this psalm. But he was also majestic. His journey to death was like a royal progress tour, ending as he was enthroned on his cross. Through 'crucified in weakness' (2 Cor. 13:4), he was displaying the power and wisdom of God (1 Cor. 1:18–31). God's majesty may have been hidden, but it was truly at work, overthrowing all oppressing powers.

Psalm 69 ✓

ORIENTATION: Predominantly a lament, this psalm is also one of the imprecatory (vengeance) psalms in which the psalmist expresses his desire to see God act in justice on his behalf.

MAP: Four themes intermingle, although there is a sense of progression in the psalm.

Trouble, 1–4, 7–12, 14–15, 19–21, 29 (NB 17)
  • It speaks of its severity.
  • It speaks of its cause, 9.

Transparency, 5
The psalmist is not asking for special favours or trying to absolve himself from responsibility. Hiding nothing from God, he believes his cause is just.

Trust, 6, 13–18, 29, 33
  • Sometimes expressed as a cry of anguished prayer.
  • Sometimes expressed as a note of confident testimony.

Triumph, 22–36
  • Justice is sought, 22–28.
  • Thanksgiving is offered, 30–33.
  • Hope is recovered, 34–36.

LINKS: Verses 9 and 21 are used to describe the experience of Jesus in John 2:17; 19:28–29.

SIGNPOST: Martin Luther confessed his need of a firm discipline in prayer, or else he admitted he would pray as the fancy took him. The devotional life he commended to others was based on the Lord's Prayer, the Ten Commandments and the Creed. He recommended that each clause should be turned into meditation by using the structure of instruction (What does it teach me?), thanksgiving (What can I thank God for?), confession (What sin should I confess?) and petition (What should I pray for?). This 'garland of four strands', he said, 'wove together a delightful crown of praise to God'. Psalm 69 is one of intense lament and anger, but if we meditate on it using Luther's structure, it will yield far more than the negative thoughts that might present themselves at first.

Seekers

ORIENTATION: The thrust of this short psalm lies in the contrast between two groups of seekers: those who seek harm and those who seek God. It is marked by urgency at the beginning and the end. Verse 1 speaks of the urgency of time. Verse 5 repeats this, but stresses the urgency of need.

MAP: The urgency of this psalm does not mean it was composed in haste, for it was evidently crafted with care.

The psalmist seeks God's help, 1
Those who seek destructive ways, 2–3
- are intent on evil;
- are destined for shame.

Those who seek God's ways, 4
- must be intent on God;
- must be confident in faith.

The psalmist seeks God's help, 5

LINKS: The psalm is virtually the same as 40:13–17. It is also said to be a very brief version of the core of the previous psalm. The mocking words 'Aha! Aha!' in v. 3 have often been compared with the mockery received by Jesus on the cross. Hence many churches read this psalm during Holy Week.

SIGNPOST: After decades when sociologists argued for the theory of secularization, which claimed that religion was in terminal decline, many are now arguing that our world is characterized not by secularism, but by religious seekership. Having lost traditional faith, people are on a quest for 'god' or the 'divine' and looking in a range of fresh, and sometimes surprising, directions. Even those who come to more traditional faith shun the confident and certain tones of previous generations and are marked by a more diffident spirit in which seeking, rather than finding, is more typical. But Jesus gives the assurance that those who genuinely seek will find (Matt. 7:7). The first step to doing so is to 'seek' in another sense – the sense in which it is used in this psalm – meaning to make something your ambition. God does not play a game of spiritual hide and seek with us. He can be found through Jesus and will be found by all who 'seek first his kingdom and his righteousness' rather than the lesser things of life (Matt. 6:33). Live in faith, making the kingdom your ambition, and you will find.

'I'm hurting': Personal lament

The Psalms reveal a raw honesty in their speaking to God. They do not hide the feelings of the worshippers, nor stifle any complaint when they feel God has let them down. A large group of psalms, especially in the first two books (1 – 72), bemoan the psalmists' experience of life and express grief over their circumstances. They are examples of what Brueggemann calls 'psalms of disorientation', psalms when life seems to be falling apart and when, as a result, faith sometimes doesn't seem to stack up.

The situations that give rise to lament are chiefly sickness (e.g., 6, 13, 22, 30, 38, 41, 88, 91) or accusation, hostility and conflict (e.g., 3, 4, 5, 7, 11, 17, 26, 27, 35, 57 and 63). Psalm 22 would be among the best-known songs of lament, but Psalm 38 is the purest example of the former and Psalm 26 of the latter. The problems that give rise to many of the psalms are more mixed.

Although there is no rigid format, these psalms frequently follow a pattern of:

- a personal petition is presented requesting a hearing;
- the trouble is described;
- a complaint is uttered;
- a request for relief is made;
- the request is supported by reasons, based on God's character;
- expressions of trust and confidence in God are voiced;
- vows are made and thanksgiving is promised.

These psalms strongly affirm the unity of our nature as human beings. Physical sickness, psychological stress, broken relationships and spiritual anguish often merge into one. One aspect has an effect on another and the psalmists speak to God about the whole of life, not just its spiritual dimension.

The spirituality they model is rare today, since we are often encouraged to bury our laments, smothering them with the sound of praise, rather than voice them. Here we have permission to 'pour out our souls to God', telling him robustly our puzzles and problems, and they provide us with language that we might use to express what otherwise we might find it hard to put into coherent words. They also usually encourage us to move beyond complaint to trust and to keep our confidence in God alive.

Psalm 71

 ORIENTATION: Central to this psalm are the repeated requests of vv. 9–11 and 17–18, in which the author asks God not to abandon him in his old age. He has experienced faith since childhood, but now confronts the (typical?) fears of the elderly. In his case it has to do with the plotting of enemies. But the enemies for many older people are the enemies of the mind and the emotions: fear, anxiety, a sense of failure, depression, frustration and physical limitations. They too cry, 'O God, don't set me aside!' (NLT)

MAP: The psalm has three movements:

Desperation in the present, 1–4
The accent falls on 'let me *never* be put to shame', 1.

Memories of the past, 5–11, 17–18
The psalmist recalls his trust in God since his earliest days.

Longings for the future, 12–16, 19–24
- a longing for freedom from enemies, 12–14;
- a longing for testimony to be given, 15–16, 22–24;
- a longing for comfort in the present, 19–21;
- a longing for God to remain faithful, 22–24.

SIGNPOST: Why is it that many Christians falter before they reach the finishing tape? Some begin their Christian life with the energy of the short-distance sprinter, but fail to pace themselves for what becomes a long-distance race. Others run well, but flag as the finishing line comes into view. The advance of years brings its own limitations and worries and can cause some who have served Christ well to take their eyes off him and become preoccupied with self. Like the psalmist, we must aim to run well, maintain a vigorous testimony and pray that we know God's presence to the last. Gordon MacDonald's recipe, in *A Resilient Life* (Nelson, 2006), for knowing our best years with Christ in our later decades is to think strategically about tomorrow, repair our pasts where they're likely to have a negative influence, manage our routines intentionally and continue to engage in rigorous self-mastery. 'Now that I am old and grey, do not abandon me, O God. Let me proclaim your power to this new generation . . . ' (v. 18, NLT).

 ORIENTATION: One of the 'royal psalms', this one may have started as David's prayer for his son Solomon (see 1 Kgs 2). If so, Solomon is only a type of the greater king to come. Christians cannot but read it as extolling the glory of the King Jesus. Watts's hymn 'Jesus Shall Reign' is based on it.

MAP: The reign of God's ideal king (Jesus) is:

Distinctive in its style, 1–7

Unlike the normal kings who rule on earth, this king refreshes rather than drains his people, and allows righteousness to flourish. The opening verses are the prelude for the themes that will be developed in the rest of the psalm.

Global in its reach, 8–11

His rule is not restricted by distance (8), indifference (9a), opposition (9b), or rivalry (10–11).

Liberating in its effect, 12–14

This reign:

- champions the cause of the vulnerable, 12–13;
- saves the weak from oppression, 14.

Prosperous in its lifestyle, 15–16

- through the wealth of the nations;
- through the resources of the earth.

Permanent in its duration, 17

Verses 18–20 are a sort of collective 'Amen' to the psalm and conclude Book II.

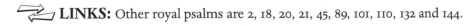 **LINKS:** Other royal psalms are 2, 18, 20, 21, 45, 89, 101, 110, 132 and 144.

SIGNPOST: Solomon's kingdom was in many respects the high point of Israel's monarchy. 1 Kgs 3 – 4 and 10:1–25 show that Psalm 72, especially vv. 8–11, were realized in him. Sadly, he failed to reach some of the psalm's other aspirations. Instead of caring for the weak and removing oppression, his many building projects imposed a new tyranny, causing rebellion and the division of his kingdom on his death. The spiritual compromises that resulted from his sexual adventures (1 Kgs 11:1–13) explain his downfall. If he was the wisest man on earth, he is a warning to us all. In Israel's mind his track record meant that there was a 'situation vacant' for an ideal king. Hence the expectation of a future messianic king, as found in Zech. 9:9–13, grew.

Psalm 73

ORIENTATION: We all struggle occasionally with the apparent injustice of the world. The wicked, who seem indifferent to anyone but themselves, prosper, while the righteous struggle. Asaph's psalm provides us with an answer when we feel like crying 'It's not fair, God'. Many consider it the hinge in the book of Psalms (see note on 'Five books or one?', p. 143).

MAP: The plot unfolds from problem, to complication, to resolution.

The problem experienced, 1–2, 13–14

It consists of:

- the fact that he believes, 1: 'God is good';
- the feeling that he experiences, 2–3: envy of the wicked;
- the frustration that he voices, 13–14: being good isn't worth it.

The wicked exposed, 4–12

They are:

- proud, 4–7;
- prosperous, 4–5, 12;
- popular, 10;
- but pagan, 9, 11.

The answer explained, 15–28

The psalmist deals with the problem by discovering:

- a new discipline, 15: he curbs his tongue;
- a new perspective, 16–17: a divine, eternal one;
- a new understanding, 18–20: the vulnerability of the wicked;
- a new self-understanding, 21–22: about his sin;
- a new vision, 23–28: of God, and of what really matters in life.

LINKS: See Psalm 37.

SIGNPOST: Rembrandt's painting *The Night Watch* hangs in the Rijksmuseum in Amsterdam, or most of it does. The authorities once reduced its size, removing three people from the original. What a way to treat a Rembrandt! Cropping it made it a different picture. In Asaph's struggle with doubt, he narrowed his spiritual vision to what he saw around him. In doing so, he lost crucial elements of the picture and couldn't make sense of what was left. It's important that we deal with the full picture spiritually, including our eternal destination (v. 17). How much more tragic it is to narrow God's full salvation than to crop a Rembrandt!

 ORIENTATION: Kidner calls this a tormented psalm and entitles it 'Havoc'. Like Psalms 79 and 137, it was composed in exile and mourns the destruction of the temple. The story is told in 2 Chr. 36:15–20. It is an urgent prayer for God to rouse himself to action in the face of seemingly prolonged inactivity (vv. 1, 22–23).

MAP: God is the connecting theme in this lament.

God's name is dishonoured, 2–8
Because:
- his people are forgotten, 2;
- his temple is destroyed, 3–8.

God's silence is bewildering, 9–11
- There is no word from God: neither prophets, nor miracles.
- There is no action by God: why?

God's power is recalled, 12–17
- The voice of faith clings on, 12: 'King from long ago'.
- The memories of faith are recalled, 13–17.

God's action is sought, 18–21
- The root of the problem is analysed. The description of the problem seems very contemporary: God's name is reviled, darkness and violence are spreading and the poor are oppressed and disgraced.
- The God of the solution is sought. Their only hope is if he rises to 'defend [his] cause'.

SIGNPOST: A Baptist deacon, E. J. Westlake, was well known for saying to those facing a crisis, 'Do not doubt in the dark what you knew to be true in the light'. It was wise advice. It's foolish to forget how the furniture is laid out in a room when you walk into it at night without switching the light on. Forgetting what you saw in daylight is likely to cause bruised shins or worse! In Psalm 74, Israel is in the deep darkness of exile. But they can recall what God did before the darkness descended (vv. 12–17). His power exhibited then was not diminished because they had suffered exile now. So they call him to remember the covenant they had celebrated in the days when the light shone (v. 20). Maybe today is dark for you, but it doesn't mean that what you knew in the light wasn't true. It was. Remember those days and know that the Lord is still your King.

Psalm 75 ✓

ORIENTATION: In the previous psalm God appeared to be absent (74:9–10). Here is a strong contrast, for v. 1 proclaims that 'your Name is near': in other words, God himself is near. The rest of the psalm traces out the consequences of his nearness. But it paints no cosy picture of God as a comfort blanket. Rather, it perfectly blends his transcendence with immanence.

 MAP: We know God is near because:

He stabilizes the earth, 2–3
- even when all seems uncertain.

He confronts the arrogant, 4–5
- even when they seem so powerful.

He determines the future, 6–7
- even when people think they're in charge.

He punishes the wicked, 8
- it is this cup of wrath that Christ refers to in regard to his own crucifixion (see Mark 10:38).

He strengthens the godly, 9–10
- whatever their present experience, they will be 'lifted up'.

SIGNPOST: It may be an old preacher's story, but it makes the point. A house caught fire and its occupants were in grave danger. Most managed to escape except for one young son, trapped on the first floor. His father told him to jump and assured him that he would catch him. His arms were powerful enough to hold him. But the son, engulfed in smoke, refused, crying, 'No, I can't see you.' The father replied, 'But I can see you, and that's what matters!' After the dark agonies of the previous psalm where God's children were struggling to see him, Psalm 75 comes as an encouragement and assures them that he can see them. He is the God who is 'near' (v. 1), not distant. The psalm then details the strong qualities of their God. Surely he would be able to rescue and uphold them, even though they couldn't see him. Jas 4:8 invites us to 'Come near to God', then assures us, 'and he will come near to you'.

'We're hurting': Community lament

Some laments are intensely personal. Others are no less intense, but voice the sorrow of the whole community or nation. Psalm 74 is a prime example. Other clear examples are found in 44, 79, 80 and 83. But there are many more psalms, like 58, 77, 85, 90, 94, 123 and 137, that incorporate elements of lament.

Each of these psalms arises from national tragedy, which is nearly always a military defeat and the experience of the consequences. The overthrow of the nation by the Babylonians and the experience of the exile are the prime illustrations of this. As with the individual laments, there are common elements in these psalms. In the following outline the verses in brackets refer to Psalm 74 by way of illustration. They:

- state the problem (1–8);
- mount a complaint against God (9–11);
- express trust in him (12–17);
- request action from him (1–3, 18–21);
- point to God as the solution to their problem (18–23);
- vow to offer praise (21);
- and appeal for his intervention (2–3, 22–23).

The most extended community lament is found in Lamentations, which complements the laments in the Psalms that concern the exile.

Community laments demonstrate that ancient Israel was characterized by much more solidarity and less individualism than contemporary Western society. Yet many nations have found them to give voice to their feelings of despair when they have been attacked and ravaged by their enemies. Care, of course, needs to be taken in using them in this way, for contemporary nations are not identical to Israel, who were the elect in a special covenant with God. We should not assume that God is on our side. But then Israel were wrong to make that presumption having failed to keep the covenant, as they discovered. Nonetheless, these psalms legitimately provide powerful words for any community in times of desolation and can lead them closer to the Creator God who is sovereign over all nations.

Psalm 76

ORIENTATION: Many see this psalm as a song celebrating the defeat of Sennacherib's army in King Hezekiah's day. See the full story in 2 Kgs 18:13 – 19:37. Others, however, see it as a more routine celebration of God's kingship associated with a New Year festival. Note particularly v. 10.

 MAP: The psalm speaks of an awesome God who is:

Famous in Jerusalem, 1–3

Majestic in light, 4

Victorious in battle, 5–6

Fearsome in judgment, 8–10

Rich in tribute, 11–12

SIGNPOST: Verse 10 makes the boldest claim of all about God: he can never be outmanoeuvred. All human attempts to outflank him end up serving his purposes and leading to his praise. The latter part of v. 10 should probably speak of God 'girding' himself with the remainder of his wrath – that is, wearing and using it rather than restraining it. It adds to the bold claim of God's incontrovertible rule. People express their anger against God not only by attacking his people, but often by blaming him for misfortune or suffering. It has become popular in some modern theologies, especially after the Holocaust, to argue that God is accountable to his creation. But this strongly asserts that God is not to be held to account by his creation; rather, they are held accountable to him. Jer. 18:1–23 and Rom. 9 – 11 provide powerful commentaries on this verse. But the clearest demonstration of its truth is found in the crucifixion of Jesus Christ, when God turned people's wrath to his praise. Spurgeon wrote of it, 'Human breath of threatening is but blowing the trumpet of the Lord's eternal fame. Let men and devils rage as they may, they cannot do otherwise than subserve the divine purposes.'

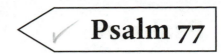

ORIENTATION: We do not know what provoked this psalm, but it is one of deep emotions, beginning with despair and ending in joy. It may best be understood using a medical analogy as a framework.

MAP: Note how the 'I' at the beginning of the psalm gives way to the 'You' at the end.

Symptoms, 1–6

He experiences:

- severe trouble, 1;
- deep depression, 2;
- near exhaustion, 3;
- morbid introspections, 4;
- condemning memories, 5–6: the songs of the past only initially add to the agony of the present and result in a misdiagnosis.

Misdiagnosis, 7–9

The original false diagnosis of his condition was that:

- God's presence has gone, 7–8a;
- God's words are empty, 8b;
- God's love is over, 9.

Cure, 5–6, 10–20

The remedy lies in regaining a true perspective with the help of a re-examination of his memories of times past and so of:

- the ways of God, 10–12: 'I will remember the deeds of the Lord . . .'
- the character of God, 13: 'holy';
- the power of God, 15, as redeemer;
- the activity of God, 16–19, in creation;
- the tenderness of God, 20, as shepherd.

SIGNPOST: Over the years we have had several pictures reframed. It's amazing what that can do to help you see them in an entirely different light. Artists know the importance of frames. They help exclude what is irrelevant, draw the eye to what is central and highlight features to their best advantage. Get the wrong frame and a picture can be sunk! So it is spiritually. Our struggles with God need to be framed in the right way. Psalm 77, like Psalm 73, is a lament that verbalizes doubt. Psalm 73:17 framed the discussion in the light of eternity. Psalm 77 frames it in the light of past history. Verses 15–19 echo Exod. 15, Miriam's song and the earliest psalm. Make sure you use the right framework when confronting doubts, or you may not see the real truth.

Fond memories of songs in the night

ORIENTATION: This amazingly rich psalm contains many individual gems (see e.g. vv. 6, 72) while rehearsing Israel's history to demonstrate how slow they were to learn God's ways. Yet his redemption always triumphed.

 MAP: A brief overview looks like this:

So the next generation might know, 1–8
These verses stress the importance of retelling the story.

The foolish example of Ephraim, 9–10
These verses allude to Exod. 1 and Num. 20. 'Ephraim' came to be a term for the ten northern tribes who broke away from Judah.

The tragic example of Israel in the wilderness, 11–29
God:

- delivered them, 12–13;
- fed them, 15–16;
- disciplined them, 30–33;
- led them, 14;
- heard them, 17–19;
- redeemed them, 34–39.

The powerful example of Israel in Egypt, 40–55
Israel soon forgot the miracles of their deliverance.

The stubborn example of Israel in the Promised Land, 56–72
Even once they had entered the land promised to them:

- their rebellion continued, 56–58;
- God's discipline continued, 59–64;
- but his redemption triumphed, 65–72, as the covenant hope reasserted itself.

SIGNPOST: Israel taught their children, so that the next generation would know the stories of old and the ways of God (vv. 4–5). They did it by telling stories and by eating the Passover and Sabbath meals. Chief Rabbi Jonathan Sacks said of this, 'I was being helped to learn who I was and the history of the people of whom I was a part. I was discovering the values that sustained my ancestors in tough times: trust, a passion for freedom and justice, a willingness to ask and learn' (*From Optimism to Hope*, Continuum, 2004). Have Christians had a failure of nerve in this regard? We entertain our children, but do we fail to teach them? The memory loss of biblical stories is horrendous in generations under forty. Should we rediscover confidence in retelling the stories and the story of our faith? If so, what are you going to do about it?

5/2/14 ✓

Psalm 79

God of our salvation

ORIENTATION: With Psalms 74 and 137, this psalm is written in the light of the fall of Jerusalem, the destruction of the temple and the exile. The reference to Asaph, one of David's musicians, possibly refers to 'the musical school or style of Asaph', since no contemporary disaster fits his age.

MAP: The psalm moves from 'they', vv. 1–3, through 'we', v. 4, to 'you', vv. 5–13.

Lamentation 1–4

- the place is defiled;
- the people are killed;
- desolation is experienced;
- scorn is encountered.

Protestation, 5–15

Here is an urgent cry, 5, for:

- nations to be judged, 6–7;
- forgiveness to be shown, 8;
- honour to be restored, 9–10;
- salvation to be granted, 11–12;
- praise to be restored, 13.

SIGNPOST: Do we suffer for wrong done by previous generations? In Psalm 79:8 Israel asks God not to 'hold against us the sins of past generations'. Some hold to the idea that punishment for sins committed in the past is meted out on subsequent generations and therefore call for present generations to identify themselves with those past sins and repent of them. In recent days many have approached the abomination of slavery in this way. Neh. 1:6 seems to be a precedent for accepting this and the saying, 'The parents have eaten sour grapes, and the children's teeth are set on edge', quoted in Jer. 31:29 and Ezek. 18:2, seems to support it. But both Jeremiah and Ezekiel rebut the saying and declare that God will not hold people accountable for the sins of previous generations, but only for their own sins (Jer. 31:29–30; Ezek. 18:1–20). What this psalm has in mind is likely to be something more indirect. Previous generations sinned and in doing so led the next generation away from God and nurtured them in bad habits and wicked living. Consequently they were suffering. But under the new covenant, as Ezek. 18:21–23 announces, when any generation turns from wickedness and starts to live obediently before God, those past sins are not held against them.

Psalm 80 ✓

 ORIENTATION: This lament on behalf of the community seems to have a threefold structure, although some scholars would question this. The prayer for restoration is addressed to the 'Shepherd of Israel' and asks for the Aaronic blessing (Num. 6:22–27) to descend once more.

 MAP: The same request comes three times:

Restore us, 3–6
> • because of the length of your discipline.

Restore us, 7–13
> • because of the evidence of your election (see Isa. 5:1–7).

Restore us, 14–19
> • because of the peril of our condition.

This section begins with 'Return to us, God Almighty!' and ends with 'Restore us, Lord God Almighty'. It continues the earlier theme of election and the metaphor of the vine, but takes them to a new level.

SIGNPOST: The sad picture of Israel broken down and in need of restoration could apply to many periods during the church's history. But God has frequently been gracious enough to restore and revive his people even when their case looked hopeless. In 1734 in Northampton, Massachusetts, a revival was ignited under the ministry of Jonathan Edwards who, worried about the moral and spiritual state of his parish, visited every home and preached a series of sermons on the gospel. A great transformation occurred and before long Edwards could write, 'The minds of the people were wonderfully taken off from the world . . . the only thing in their view was to get into the Kingdom of Heaven, and everyone appeared pressing into it . . . The work of conversion was carried on in the most astonishing manner.' Soon the revival flames spread across the Atlantic and God used George Whitefield and John Wesley to transform the fortunes of a dying church. The backbone of it all, as they document and as this psalm illustrates, was desperate believing prayer which pleaded with God to act. Do we not need to be praying for restoration and revival today?

'Blot out my transgressions'

A group of psalms have long been recognized as penitential psalms, or the 'Songs of the Sinner'. They are 6, 32, 38, 51, 102, 130 and 143. In one sense they are a special form of lament song, as the psalmist laments his own failure in relation to God. They are not the only psalms to talk of sin, but the concept of sin is expressed profoundly within them. Other situations and people are not involved. These psalms are a one-to-one between God and the sinner.

The psalms use a variety of Hebrew words to describe sin (translated as 'sin', 'sins', 'transgression', 'wickedness' and 'iniquity'), but the penitential psalms see it primarily as an offence against God that arises from a universal and inherent flaw in the human condition (51:5; 143:2). That, however, does not absolve the sinner from responsibility for it. It remains a personal choice and act of one's will, even sometimes an act of outright rebellion.

Sin brings a number of consequences in its train, as each of the penitential psalms notes, including physical sickness, psychological distress, personal unhappiness, broken relationships and spiritual defilement (6:2–3, 6–10; 32:3–4; 38:3–8, 10–12; 51:7–12; 102:3–11; 130:1; 143:3–4).

The solution to sin and to overcoming its painful consequences is extremely simple and profoundly difficult at the same time. It lies in owning the responsibility for sin and confessing one's guilt before God (32:5). Excusing it, justifying it and arguing about mitigating circumstances hinder God from dealing with it by blotting it out (51:1, 9). Recognizing guilt and casting oneself on God's mercy is the only hope (6:2, 9; 51:1; 130:2–8; 143:1). So simple, yet how we wriggle and protest in self-justification and out of self-preservation.

What relief is experienced once confession is made, as Psalms 32 and 51 testify in particular. But forgiveness is not quite the end of the matter. Forgiveness brings with it renewed responsibilities to walk obediently with God (143:10) and to teach others his ways (51:10).

The Psalms are never blasé about sin, but nonetheless administer a sweet medicine for it without explaining in full how God can offer forgiveness and maintain his righteousness. For that we look to the cross of Christ.

Psalm 81

ORIENTATION: Verse 3 implies that this psalm was part of the liturgy during the climax of Israel's year and New Moon festivals, but it may be used more widely as a reflection on worship, especially when life is tough. Brueggemann says it reflects 'disorientation' in which 'Israel is expected to listen as much as speak' and to hear things from God's viewpoint. As the seasons conjure up different moods, so this psalm reflects the different moods found in rounded worship.

MAP: The seasons are outlined:
Summer: worship as rejoicing, 1–5
- joyful acts of celebration, 1–3;
- joyful obedience to God's commands, 4–5: his decrees, ordinance and statutes.

Autumn: worship as remembering, 6–10
- God's deliverance, 6–7a;
- God's discipline, 7: see Exod. 17:1–7;
- God's demands, 8–10.

Winter: worship as repenting, 11–16
- God's pain, 11–12;
- God's plea, 13: 'if my people would only listen';
- God's promise, 14–16.

Brueggemann writes, 'The wonder of Yahweh and the news of this psalm is that Israel is again invited to *hear* . . . Yahweh does not want Israel left to its fate. Yahweh is ready to move on to a new life together. There is no need for lingering punishment.' So, after winter, spring may come again.

SIGNPOST: Some experience the Christian life as one of equanimity, but most have a less steady relationship with God than that. We may feel guilty for the unevenness of our experience, but perhaps there is another way of looking at it. Healthy relationships involve change. If they were the same all the time they would probably die of boredom! Seasons have their value. They show that periods of fruitfulness require periods of quiet preparation and recovery. Where there is perpetual sun, all you get is desert. So with our Christian lives. Cultivate and enjoy the varying seasons of your relationship with God, without guilt. Look back at the seasons you have been through. Have an awareness of the season you are in right now. But remember, one season should give way to another. Don't use it as an excuse to get stuck in a perpetual autumn or winter.

 ORIENTATION: While the major part of this psalm concerns human judges, it begins and ends with God, the divine Judge, to whom all human judges are accountable. The God who presides in the court of judges is defender and rescuer of the weak.

MAP: A guide to the heavenly court is provided.

The supreme Judge, 1, 8
God, as the supreme Judge to whom all others are accountable:
  • presides in his court in the present, 1;
  • and will preside in his court in the future, 8.

The human judges, 2–7
Human judges are:
  • challenged, 2: 'How long?'
  • reminded, 3–4, of their responsibilities;
  • accused, 5, of ignorance and failure;
  • humbled, 6–7: they may be powerful now, but they are mortal like anyone else.

SIGNPOST: I was once invited to lunch with the judges at the Old Bailey. It was a somewhat daunting experience as twenty of them sat around the table in their ermine-laced robes discussing the law. It was also somewhat comic for me, since I'd had an accident a few days before and turned up in bandages, looking like someone who belonged in the dock rather than at the lunch table! But I discovered how human they were. It wasn't long before family matters, hobbies and ordinary stories surfaced in conversation. The administration of justice is a major concern in the Bible. It is especially concerned that the poor and vulnerable are defended (see v. 3). No society can be healthy if justice is corrupt, maladministered or biased towards the rich and powerful. Judges may appear awesome, but they are ordinary people, subject to pressures and temptations like the rest of us. Pray for them that in their role true and honest justice may be administered. And, if you are available, seek ways in which you can get involved in victim support, as a mentor or as a prison visitor.

Psalm 83

ORIENTATION: Asaph was David's worship leader (1 Chr. 16:7, 37). A collection of his poems has been included in the Psalms (or a collection of poems by his followers composed after his style). The collection began with Psalm 73 and this one brings it to an end. Wilcox says that this 'is far more likely to mean a climax than an unimportant tailpiece'.

 MAP: The psalm essentially asks three things of God:

Hear the tumult, Lord, 1–8
The clamour consists of:
- the enemies' growling tone, 2–3;
- the enemies' destructive word, 4;
- the enemies' mounting conspiracy, 5–8.

Do it again, Lord, 9–12
Recalling God's judgment on previous enemies, the psalmist asks God to treat the contemporary opposition in the same way.

Blow them away, Lord, 13–18
Using the imagery of a furious gale, the psalmist asks that the enemies might be revealed for the flimsy, insubstantial 'chaff' they are. The wind image continues as the fanning of a terrifying forest fire. Verse 8 states the motive for all this: so that they might learn 'that you alone are the Most High over all the earth'.

SIGNPOST: At the height of the Iraq war, a group of American Christians took out newspaper advertisements in support of US troops with the headline 'Blow them away, in the name of the Lord!', echoing Psalm 83:15. But we should be careful about hijacking scripture for our own nationalistic or political ends. Before applying any psalm directly to our situation, we should ask what it originally meant and to whom it originally referred. This psalm is about God's chosen people, Israel, who were under attack. No nation now stands in covenant with God as Israel did, so none can claim these words directly for themselves. Asaph asks God to intervene. And we should pray for God to act against all wickedness and judge *his* enemies (see v. 2), especially when Christians are persecuted. Given this, and Jesus' command to 'love your enemies' (Matt. 5:44), we dare not usurp scriptures like these and make them a pretext for our own wars today.

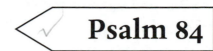

Psalm 84

ORIENTATION: Each year pilgrims from all over Israel made their way to Jerusalem for the great festivals. This is one of the songs the pilgrims would have sung on their journey and reflects their impatience to arrive (v. 2).

MAP: The psalm has three movements:

Thirsting for God, 1–4

Because the God they worship is:

- almighty, 1, 3, 8, 12;
- living, 2b, in contrast to dead idols;
- gentle, 3–4, even with sparrows and swallows.

Strengthened by God, 5–9

On the journey, God's strength is:

- a progressive strength, 5, 7: enabling the pilgrims to go towards their destination;
- a transforming strength, 6: pilgrims transform for the better the barren places (Valley of Baka) through which they pass;
- a selective strength, 9: available to those among the covenant people of Jacob who pray.

Delighting in God, 10–12

The delight is:

- expressed, 10;
- explained, 11;
- exclaimed, 12.

SIGNPOST: In the world in which I live, hunger is virtually unknown. On the odd occasion when I say 'I'm famished', I'm really nothing of the sort in comparison with the genuine hunger a third of our world knows. Sadly, my hunger for God can be of the 'I'm famished' type: true, but only to a paltry extent. Here the pilgrims show a real desire to meet with God and enjoy being in his presence. They have a hunger for him. How hungry am I for God? How hungry am I to enjoy his perpetual presence? Perhaps my trouble is that I hunger too much for other things. Modern culture is good at filling us with junk food and cheap substitutes for a nourishing and healthy relationship with God. Jesus said, 'Blessed are those who hunger and thirst for righteousness, for they will be filled' (Matt. 5:6). 'Lord, help me to cultivate a real hunger and mature appetite for you and not be satisfied with the spiritual junk food that gives me a quick but unhealthy fix.'

ORIENTATION: Reflecting on the way God had restored Israel before, this psalm, probably written in exile, asks God to restore them again (vv. 4–5). But the striking thing is the amazing juxtaposition of qualities attributed to God's salvation in vv. 10–11 which are the basis of our hope. Here are qualities, usually considered to be in conflict, or which are bound to repel each other, that God holds in perfect balance.

MAP: Here is a close-up of vv. 10–11.

Love and truth, 10a
The TNIV has 'faithfulness'. Sometimes when we know the truth about someone we no longer want to love them or be faithful to them. But here is covenant love 'that will not let us go'.

Righteousness and peace, 10b
Righteousness would often result, we think, in punishment, not peace. But these twin qualities are reconciled in the cross of Christ: that's where they meet. Consequently so do:

Heaven and earth, 11
As Tom Wright writes in *Simply Christian* (London: SPCK, 2006, p. 56f.), 'The Old Testament insists that God belongs in heaven and we on earth. Yet it shows over and over again that the two spheres do indeed overlap, so that God makes his presence known, seen and heard within the sphere of the earth.'

SIGNPOST: 'Are we there yet?' Most parents have been driven mad by that question when the journey has only just begun. This psalm knows Israel hasn't yet reached home and smacks of the same urgency as the child's question. Still in exile, Israel understands that going home is going to take a miracle. But God has done it before and they believe he will do it again (vv. 4, 6). Such is their anticipation that vv. 10–12 speak as if they've already arrived and are enjoying God's goodness. There's something about going home that isn't matched by any other experience in life. Our true home still lies in the future, in a city 'with foundations, whose architect and builder is God' (Heb. 11:10), where God dwells among his people (Rev. 21:3). Let the anticipation of going home inspire you with hope and perseverance while you are still on the journey.

The perfect balance

'Curse them, Lord': Psalms of vengeance

Most of us find the inclusion of a number of psalms of vengeance very uncomfortable. How can they be included right alongside psalms that have such holy and uplifting thoughts? And how can they use such ferocious language to describe what the poet would love to happen to his enemies (see 109:6–20 as just one example)? Yet they're there – included in inspired Scripture. Such psalms include 35, 59, 69, 70, 109, 137 and 140.

While this is not the place for a full answer, a few pointers may be given. First, the presence of these psalms testifies to the honesty of the book of Psalms. It has not been sanitized, but truly reflects all of life's experiences and often does so in the raw. Anger is part of life and the Psalms would have something of a fictional quality if it was not to be found there.

Second, rather than denying it, it is much healthier to express our anger and to do so to God, rather than to others. It is evident that, in praying as he does, David, or whoever is writing, is refusing to take the law into his own hands and wants God to take action. He never says to God, 'I'm going to smash their head in,' but rather, 'Lord, *you* smash their head in.' The grievance is given over to God for him to deal with, just as Rom. 12:19 instructs us to do.

Third, we should be aware that the anger expressed here is not a fit of temper, but judicious anger. Apart from Psalm 137, which relates to the exile, the other psalms are all psalms of David and relate to his calling as king of Israel. As king, or future king, he should have been concerned about the wickedness that would undermine his position and nation. C. S. Lewis commented that these psalms were written 'at least in part because they took right and wrong more seriously' than we do. He went on, 'Thus the absence of anger, especially that sort of anger which we call indignation can, in my opinion, be a most alarming symptom. And the presence of indignation may be a good one.' It recognizes that wickedness is offensive to God.

The reader is referred to the *Signposts* in Psalms 58, 94 and 109 for additional comment.

Psalm 86 ✓

ORIENTATION: This psalm covers familiar territory. It consists of several petitions, mostly using phrases found in David's earlier psalms. But note v. 17, 'Give me a sign of your goodness', or 'Send me a sign of your favour' (NLT).

MAP: Overall, David petitions God on the basis of his covenant (vv. 1–4); his character (vv. 5–7); his incomparability (vv. 8–10); his salvation (vv. 11–13) and his compassion (vv. 14–17). Here we focus in a more detailed map on v. 17.

The request

The request sounds self-centred, a plea for special consideration, but the context makes it look different:

- the request is wrung out of desperation and conflict, 1–7, 14;
- the request is founded on the person of God (see above);
- the request is coupled with a plea to keep in step with God, 11–12.

Yet it remains specific and bold.

The reason

What motivates it is that 'my enemies may . . . be put to shame', 17b. This sounds vindictive and self-justifying. Perhaps so, but these people should feel shame, for 'they have no regard for' God (see NLT) and this means they behave insolently and ruthlessly. God's favour is needed so the community might know that God is God.

The rationale

The request is premised on the character of God, who has been extolled in vv. 1–10 as merciful, good, forgiving, listening, unique, creating and powerful.

SIGNPOST: It's often said that the OT God is not a very attractive one. He's demanding, warlike, vengeful and punitive – in contrast to the loving God in the NT. But this is profoundly to misread the OT God and would be a surprising picture to David and most other OT figures. Psalm 86:15 quotes Exod. 34:6 – a fundamental passage revealing God to be 'compassionate and gracious . . . slow to anger, abounding in love', who maintains love to thousands and forgives sin, yet whose patience can run out. This Exodus revelation is quoted eight times in the OT, including in Psalms 86:15; 103:8 and 145:8. What image do you have of God? How does Exod. 34:6–7 shape your image? Is he less stern and more compassionate than you think? Is your relationship with him a warm one, like David's?

 ORIENTATION: This simple and unashamed celebration of Jerusalem trumpets the qualities of Zion, the 'city of God', because it 'symbolizes God's kingdom presence' (VanGemeren).

 MAP: The 'tourist's guide' comments on:

The glorious city, 1–3
Consider:

- its divine origin, 1;
- its divine favour, 2;
- its divine presence, 3.

It is God's presence, rather than anything else, that makes it special.

The glorious citizens, 4–7
Consider:

- their multinational identity, 4;
- their spiritual rebirth, 5;
- their secure inheritance, 6;
- their life-giving worship, 7.

 LINKS: This psalm anticipates a number of NT developments:
- It exemplifies an international church (Eph. 2:11–22; Gal. 3:28).
- It hints at the need for spiritual birth (John 3:1–8).
- It anticipates the Lamb's book of life (Rev. 20:12, 15; 21:27).
- It foresees the city of the living God (Heb. 12:18–24; Rev. 21 – 22).

SIGNPOST: I was walking across the Sydney Harbour Bridge with a friend. As we looked over to the famous Opera House he said, 'This is my city. I was born here, belong here, know how it works and I'm proud of it. It's wonderful.' Most of us boast about the places where we grew up and love to show people the sites that mean so much to us. Citizens of Jerusalem had a special reason for doing so. It was a unique city. But it was to reach its 'sell-by' date and give way to the new Jerusalem which, in some ways, is still to come. Yet Paul boasts that 'our citizenship is in heaven' (Phil. 3:20). Already we belong to that great city. What does it mean to do so? How does this city tick? Do we live according to its customs and laws? Do we take pride in belonging?

Glorious things are said of you

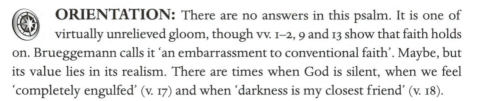

Psalm 88

ORIENTATION: There are no answers in this psalm. It is one of virtually unrelieved gloom, though vv. 1–2, 9 and 13 show that faith holds on. Brueggemann calls it 'an embarrassment to conventional faith'. Maybe, but its value lies in its realism. There are times when God is silent, when we feel 'completely engulfed' (v. 17) and when 'darkness is my closest friend' (v. 18).

MAP: Here we read of:
The darkness of near death, 3–5
The darkness of God's wrath, 6–9
Characterized by:
- the darkest depths;
- the denial of friendships;
- the daily crying.

The darkness of future oblivion, 10–12
Death, as opposed to life, means being cut off from God 'in the place of darkness'.
The darkness of unanswered prayer, 13–14
He prays, but only to face rejection.
The darkness of deep despair, 15–18
- his suffering has been prolonged;
- his suffering has been all-consuming.

SIGNPOST: There are times when, no matter what we do, God seems to be absent and there are no answers. They may be times of fierce temptation, spiritual attack, evil, illness or suffering. Psalm 88 was composed about just such a time. The psalmist complains, 'Why, Lord, do you reject me and hide your face from me?' In his pastoral advice to others, Martin Luther spoke much about 'the hiddenness of God', which he had experienced within his own life. He took the experience of God's absence seriously and refused to rush to superficial solutions. He admitted that this was 'strong wine' and not for young Christians. But it led him to understand that God calls some to a deep faith that holds on in the darkness when no resolution seems near, and that the God in whom we trust is the God who made himself known in the hiddenness of Christ's cross. This deep paradox where the hidden yet revealed God is seen in Christ's suffering is sometimes mirrored in our own experience. The deep darkness calls for deep faith that yields eventually to a deep experience of the God of glory. That's why Luther called it 'delicious despair'.

 ORIENTATION: The very positive beginning to this psalm cannot stop it from being chiefly an expression of disappointment. The security of David's throne was thought to be guaranteed (see 2 Sam. 7), but now seemed under threat. So what does God's 'for ever' mean?

MAP: The plot of this psalm involves:

The prologue, 1–4
The foundation for praise lies in God's promise to David to make his throne 'firm through all generations'.

The profession, 5–8
The initial praise expands into a confession of faith in:

- the scope of God's cosmic rule, 5–7;
- the uniqueness of God's faithful rule, 8;
- the power of God's creation rule, 9–13;
- the justice of God's kingly rule, 14–18.

The promise, 19–37
These verses explore the nature of God's promise concerning the permanence of David's line. Even when David's sons lived disobediently and discipline was exercised, the dominant note is still one of love: ' . . . but I will not take my love from him, nor will I ever betray my faithfulness' (v. 33).

The problem, 38–52
What happened? Why has God gone back on his promise? Verse 49 cries: 'Lord, where is your former great love?' In this psalm there are no answers.

SIGNPOST: 'For no matter how many promises God has made, they are "Yes" in Christ. And so through him the "Amen" is spoken by us to the glory of God' (2 Cor. 1:20). The writer of Psalm 89 felt he couldn't say 'Amen' to God's promises. Have you ever felt that? You've believed that a Bible promise would come true for you and it hasn't, or you have applied Phil. 4:13 or 4:19 to yourself and then felt let down by God. Remember, the promise to David was never a blanket one. What happened to his throne was foreseen in the original covenant with God. And God was true to his promise, but fulfilled it in unexpected ways. King Jesus came to inherit David's throne. For us, God's promises aren't blanket promises, but promises 'in Christ', so they will be fulfilled in line with his ways, will and glory. We should read (and believe) God's promises in context and be cautious about neatly applying them to ourselves.

Psalm 90

ORIENTATION: No psalm contrasts the greatness of God and the fragility of humans so effectively as this one. Kidner comments, 'Only Isaiah 40 can compare with this psalm for its presentation of God's grandeur and eternity over against the frailty of man.'

MAP: In contrast to human beings, this psalm speaks of:

The eternity of God, 1–6

- God is an eternal refuge, 1.
- God is an eternal Creator, 2.
- God is the eternal Lord, 3–6.

The holiness of God, 7–12

Human transience is not an unfortunate accident, but results:

- from God's anger, 7–9, 11;
- from a fallen creation, 10;
- in a prayer for wisdom, 12.

The grace of God, 13–17

Here is a prayer:

- for God's mercy, 13;
- for God's transformation, 14–15;
- for God's intervention, 16;
- for God's approval, 17.

SIGNPOST: On one visit to the London Planetarium I saw the most stunning show. Starting with a close-up of a person's face, the satellite camera zoomed out and out until we had the image of our vast universe projected on the domed ceiling. It put us in perspective: how tiny we are! That, in effect, is what Psalm 90 does. The previous psalm was full of complaint about what God was doing (or, rather, not doing). The writer's horizon was filled by the problem he was facing. Psalm 90 zooms back and puts his problem into a much larger perspective – the perspective of the God who has been their dwelling place 'throughout all generations'. If God had cared for them all that time, would he not now care for them in their present troubles? And if God was as awesome as the psalm claims, would he not be able to deal with their little local difficulty? We sometimes think too much of ourselves and our problems fill our own horizons. Let's get ourselves into perspective. Let's zoom out, see how small we, and our problems, are and how great is the God in whom we trust.

'Teach me your ways, Lord':
Wisdom psalms

A group of psalms share the concerns and perspectives of the Wisdom literature of the OT, namely of Proverbs, Ecclesiastes and Job. They vary enormously in style, from short, punchy teaching psalms (e.g. 1, 127), to those that incorporate proverbs (e.g. 32:6–8), to long, reflective meditations (e.g. 73, 119). Most agree that 1, 25, 32, 34, 37, 49, 73, 112, 119, 127, 128 and 133 fall into this category, although there is a lot of disagreement about which other ones do. A subgroup within this category is particularly concerned about the teaching of the law (1, 19, 119).

Wisdom literature itself is quite varied and this is reflected in the psalms. Proverbs is concerned to give pithy advice about how to live wisely in our everyday lives. It assumes that God has built an order into the world and that life is much easier if we go with that grain rather than cut across it. Ecclesiastes, however, is not so easily satisfied and struggles with the big question about the meaning of life. How can one live wisely in the face of the apparent absurdities of life and the number of things that seem to contradict the conventional belief of the faith community? Job, as is well known, is an extended struggle with the problem of suffering when you believe in a good and powerful God.

All these themes are found in the wisdom psalms. Psalms 1, 119 and 128, for example, are interested in the question of lifestyle; 37 and 73 deal with the enigmas we face; and 49 has similarities to the book of Job. Many other connections can be traced between the wisdom psalms and the wider Wisdom literature, including the use of similes, the structure 'blessed are . . . ', and even the practice of addressing the readers as 'children'. As in Proverbs, some are marked by a sense of justice and a firm belief that the wicked will receive just retribution.

The overall thrust of these psalms might be summed up by 90:12: 'Teach us to number our days, that we may gain a heart of wisdom.'

Psalm 91

ORIENTATION: This is a wonderful psalm of assurance for those facing trouble. The promises found here fit with the covenant blessings set out in Lev. 26:1–13 and Deut. 28:1–14.

MAP: Four words summarize the psalm:

Confidence, 1–4
'Whoever dwells . . . '
- will rest . . . will be saved . . . will be covered;
- imagery of battle, 2, hunting, 3, and a mother hen, 4, is employed to stress security in God.

Consequence, 5–8
So there is no need to fear:
- whenever, be it morning, noon or night;
- whatever happens around you.

Condition, 9–13
'If . . . '
- active faith required;
' . . . then'
- angelic help ready;
- astonishing protection available.

Confirmation, 14–16
It is extraordinary to hear the direct voice of God, confirming his protection and his preservation of the life of whomever 'dwells in the shelter of the Most High'.

SIGNPOST: At the heart of the marriage service the bride and groom say 'I will' to each other. It is a solemn, if joyful, moment when two people covenant themselves to each other in an open and risky way. Walter Brueggemann has pointed out how often God says 'I will' to his people in this psalm of reassurance. The language of volition is used throughout, but in vv. 14–16 alone God utters his promise to Israel seven times in an explicit and intentional way. Each statement is worth meditating on. But, Brueggemann adds, 'The self-assertion of God is a response to the boldness of submission.' His promises are again (see previous *Signpost*) not blank cheques, but apply to those who submit to him. 1 Pet. 5:5–11 provides a NT commentary on this. If Israel could rejoice in God's assurance, how much more can we, the new Israel (Gal. 6:16) sing, 'Blessed assurance, Jesus is mine'?

ORIENTATION: Praise is a good thing. Spurgeon said, 'It is good ethically, for it is the Lord's right; it is good emotionally, for it is pleasant to the heart; it is good practically, for it leads others to render the same homage.' To praise regularly is better still (the title of the psalm refers to the Sabbath, but daily praise is not precluded by that!). To praise extravagantly is even better still.

 MAP: Here are some of God's perfections that call forth daily praise.

God's works, 4–5
NLT translates v. 5 as referring to miracles.

God's wisdom, 5b–7
This is profound, even though unintelligible to the wicked.

God's eternity, 8–9
He is 'for ever exalted' while his enemies perish.

God's justice, 10–11
He empowers the weak while defeating their enemies.

God's blessing, 12–15
This is seen in the flourishing and fruitful lives of the righteous, even to 'old age'. NLT translates v. 15b as 'there is nothing but goodness in him'. Spurgeon said, 'He is a friend without fault, a helper without fail.'

SIGNPOST: C. S. Lewis offered some insightful comments on the importance of praise in his *Reflections on the Psalms*, comments worth considering. He writes of three things he had never noticed: (1) 'that all enjoyment spontaneously overflows in praise unless shyness or the fear of boring others is deliberately brought in to check it'; (2) 'how the humblest, and at the same time the most balanced and capricious, minds praised most, while the cranks, misfits and malcontents praised least'; and (3) 'that just as men praise spontaneously whatever they value, so they spontaneously urge us to join in praising it'. He continued, 'I think we delight to praise what we enjoy because the praise not merely expresses but completes the enjoyment: it is its appointed consummation. It is not out of compliment that lovers keep on telling one another how beautiful they are; the delight is incomplete till it is expressed.' So it is with our praise of God.

Psalm 93 ✓

 ORIENTATION: From here to Psalm 100 (with the exception of Psalm 94?) there is a common theme celebrating God as King over all the earth. This psalm largely looks to creation as a means of stressing why God is rightfully King.

 MAP: Here we learn that the Lord's reign is characterized by:

Majesty, 1
He is a strong ruler.

Security, 1c
He is a beneficial ruler.

Eternity, 2
He is an established ruler.

Authority, 3–4
He is an orderly ruler (bringing peace out of chaos).

Energy, 3–4
He is a powerful ruler.

Morality, 5
He is a holy ruler.

SIGNPOST: The Psalms that proclaim God as King make bold assertions that often, on the face of it, seem contradicted by experience. If God reigns supreme, why does nature threaten chaos, suffering continue and the enemy triumph? These declarations are made in faith. Their faith is not groundless, wishful thinking. It is based on a good foundation, which is why they constantly look back to creation and the grand picture story of Israel. But the claim that God is King is a statement of faith nonetheless. As Christians, our declaration of God's kingship is based on an even firmer foundation as we look back to the cross and the empty tomb. But the claims necessarily remain claims of faith. Christians can never dispense with faith. The evidence is never so certain that we can do away with it. It is in our DNA that 'we fix our eyes not on what is seen, but on what is unseen. For what is seen is temporary, but what is unseen is eternal' (2 Cor. 4:18). So, with the Psalmists, we can confidently proclaim that God is King.

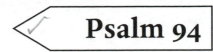
 ORIENTATION: The opening words, 'The Lord is a God who avenges', come as something of a shock. This is not our picture of God in late modernity, an age of excessive tolerance. Wilcock comments, 'Without saying so in as many words, 94 chimes with the rest of this group of psalms in proclaiming that the Lord is King.'

MAP: The psalm teaches four vital things about God:

The absence of God is something to be mourned, 1–7
Whether people believe in God or not isn't a neutral issue, as it is often considered to be, but one that has immense practical impact.

The vengeance of God is something to be avoided, 8–11
People may not believe in God, but he sees all their actions and will react accordingly.

The discipline of God is something to be welcomed, 12–15
God's correction of believers is to be distinguished from his judgment on unbelievers.

The justice of God is something to be celebrated, 16–23
In righteousness, the Lord stands up against bullies and protects the weak. He provides support for those facing extreme and unjust attack.

SIGNPOST: What sort of a God do you want? The thought of God as 'an avenging God' is not a popular one in contemporary, tolerant society and some Christians find it hard to square with their picture of a loving Jesus. But a God who never expressed anger at wickedness would surely be an unworthy God, and certainly not one to trust. Wickedness is a destructive force that reduces God's creation to chaos and subjects his people to injustice. Sadly, wickedness isn't an impersonal force and can't be divorced from those who perpetrate it. A God who was indifferent to Hitler, Pol Pot, Saddam Hussein and the thousands of lesser perpetrators of evil would be contemptible. This isn't just the OT picture of God. The Bible consistently speaks of him standing in judgment against evil. See Rom. 1:18; 12:19; Col. 3:6; 1 Thess. 1:10; 2 Thess. 1:5–10 for starters, and then read the book of Revelation! Thank God that he opposes wrongdoing and is a just God.

Psalm 95

ORIENTATION: The references to incidents that occurred in the wilderness (vv. 8–11) mean that this psalm has been associated with the Feast of Tabernacles. It is best to read it through the lens of v. 6, as a psalm about worship.

MAP: This psalm gives useful direction about worship.

Worship is about rejoicing, 1–2
- The rejoicing is corporate: 'Let *us* . . . let *us* . . . '
- The rejoicing is vibrant: 'sing . . . shout aloud . . . '
- The rejoicing is musical: 'with music and song' (see Col. 3:16).

Worship is about reflection, 3–7b
- On God as King, 3.
- On God as Creator, 4–5.
- On God as Shepherd, 7.

Worship is about responding, 7c–11

Worship is about responding obediently to God's voice. So the psalm presents:
- a present opportunity, 7c: 'Today' (Heb. 3:7 – 4:16 develops the text further);
- a past warning (this refers back to Exod. 17:7 and Num. 20:13, as does Psalm 81).

Having been so positive, the psalm seems to end abruptly on a somewhat negative note. As Kidner puts it, 'By ending on this note the psalm sacrifices literary grace for moral urgency.' But it is good that its stark warning about the heart in and the heart of worship is not softened.

SIGNPOST: Patterns of worship have changed enormously in recent decades as new forms of service, new patterns of leadership and new technologies have emerged to channel the creative explosion of music and song that has taken place. The church's energy has often been exhausted by discussions (and arguments) about worship. But biblical teaching about worship is clear. Take the four key passages of this psalm, Isa. 58, Amos 5:21–24 and Rom. 12:1–2 and listen to the harmony that emerges. What we sing in church is not the issue. How we live our lives outside the church is. The worship God requires is one of submission to his word. As living sacrifices available completely to God, we will be distinguished by lives of prompt obedience, moral purity, gospel passion and social justice.

A quick reference guide

Although we need to be careful about taking verses out of context and applying them neatly to ourselves, there are many times when God uses his word to give us immediate encouragement and direction, or when individual verses give us words to express our needs. Here is a quick reference guide to use when looking for help in a variety of circumstances.

	Psalm(s)
Anger	37:8; 69:16–36; 94; 109
Anxiety	3; 91; 94:19; 121
Assurance, of God's love	36:7; 91
Bereavement	23:4; 30; 46:1–3; 68:5–6
Broken-hearted	34:18; 147:3
Depressed	42; 43
Doubt	37; 73; 77:10–12
Envy	37; 73; 131
Failure	37:23–24
Guidance, in need of	32:8; 37:5; 119:105
God's discipline	32:4–5; 38:1–22; 94:12–13
Insecurity	37; 89:1–3; 94:17–18; 121:3
Isolation	61; 68:5–6; 139:7–12
Let down by others	55:12–22; 146
Loneliness	27:10; 38:9–22; 121
Old age	71; 90
Peace	29:11; 34:14; 85:8–13; 119:165
Persecution	9:13–14; 18; 31:9–18; 119:86
Sickness	22; 38; 41:3
Sin, confession of	32; 51; 103
Stress	62; 116:1–7
Temptation	18:30–39; 119:9, 11
Thanksgiving	66; 92; 103; 118
Trouble	22:11; 37:39; 86; 107
Trust in God	40:1–5; 55:23; 62:8; 146

Psalm 96

ORIENTATION: The story behind this psalm is found in 1 Chr. 16. The ark of the covenant is going to its rightful home, Jerusalem. The event is a sign that the Lord rules over pagan territory. Hence it emphasizes God's sovereignty over 'all the earth', the 'nations' and 'all peoples'.

MAP: This psalm changes scale to include ever-widening circles in the praise of God.

It offers an invitation to the people of God, 1–3

- to sing: not in obligation, but in celebration;
- to tell: not a dialogue, but a declaration.

It offers an explanation to the nations of earth, 4–10

Why is this God so great? Because of:

- his position, 4–5: superior to other gods;
- his person, 6–8: majesty surrounds him;
- his power, 5, 10, 13: as Creator and Judge;
- his purity, 9: holiness characterizes him.

It offers an exhortation to all elements of creation, 11–13

The whole of creation is summoned to join in rejoicing in God. God's judgment is seen, here and elsewhere, not just as calling people to account, but as 'a joyful anticipation of overcoming the disarray and disharmony in creation and setting things right' (Jannine Du Preez, quoted by Christopher Wright, *The Mission of God*, Nottingham: IVP, 2006, p. 410).

SIGNPOST: The slogan 'Think globally, act locally' has been much used by environmentalists and those seeking to overcome the world's unjust poverty. The word 'glocal' has recently been coined to emphasize how much the local and global are enmeshed with each other. What we do locally has international implications, while globalization affects us at a local level. The Bible taught the concepts long before these modern slogans. What happened in and to Jerusalem had international implications. That's why bringing the ark to Jerusalem, a joyful but local event, sparked the grand dimensions of this psalm. The nations of the earth are summoned to praise. Today it is a two-way street. Think how much your local spiritual actions of prayer, witnessing, caring for creation and doing good can affect the world. But think too how the spiritual needs and the growth of the church around the world have an impact on you. Be a glocal Christian!

 ORIENTATION: It is better for the earth that the Lord rules than that idols are in charge.

 MAP: Three semi-technical words help us chart our way through this psalm.

Theophany: God majestically appears, 1–6
Reminiscent of God's appearance on Mount Sinai (Exod. 19), these verses describe the dramatic effect on creation when its Maker appears in majestic glory.

Theism: God truly exists, 7
The folly of worshipping empty and lifeless idols is ridiculed and these tin-pot gods are summoned to worship the only truly living God who rules over all.

Theocracy: God beneficially rules, 8–12
The benefits of God's rule are extolled:
- his supremacy, 9;
- his purity, 10: his people should hate evil;
- his value, 10–11: his impact on the world is good;
- his favour, 11: 'Light shines on the righteous';
- his holiness, 12b: 'his holy name'.

SIGNPOST: Throughout the Psalms, as here, there is an acknowledgment of the existence of other gods besides the 'I AM', Yahweh, the God of Israel. The Psalms assume a range of heavenly beings and so-called deities. It accepts that people worship different idols, believe in different gods and adopt different lifestyles as a result. God is even said to hold a council of heavenly beings who serve him (82; 89:7; 103:20–21), though he is unique and pre-eminent among them. Paul took something of this same line about 'so-called gods' in discussing food offered to idols in 1 Cor. 8:4–6, though with a degree of scepticism about their actual existence. But monotheism, the belief in one real God, had been Israel's position since their earliest days (see Deut. 6:4) and throughout they affirm the indomitable supremacy of Yahweh. This position came into even clearer focus with the Prophets (see Isa. 43:10–13; 45:5, 6, 18), who saw this unique God as making radical ethical claims on his people. The high point of the doctrine is seen in 1 Tim. 2:5: one God has provided one mediator as Saviour of his one world. Look at 1 Tim. 6:13–16 and turn it into prayer.

Psalm 98

 ORIENTATION: Here is a straightforward, uncomplicated psalm of praise, starting with God and gradually embracing the whole of creation.

 MAP: Simply put, this psalm is about:

Divine proclamation, 1–3

The emphasis in these opening verses is on the Lord's activity in making known, announcing and revealing his salvation. It involves an announcement about:

- his might, 1;
- his salvation, 1d–2a;
- his righteousness, 2b;
- his faithfulness, 3;
- his sovereignty, 3b.

Human celebration, 4–6

The appropriate response is one of great celebration that includes shouting, as well as singing, and making 'a joyful symphony' to the Lord (v. 6, NLT).

Creation's acclamation, 7–8

It is not only the nations but also creation itself that joins in the adulation offered to the King.

SIGNPOST: I may be slow, but the invitation to sing 'a new song' (v. 1) used to confuse me. Psalms 33:3; 40:3; 96:1; 144:9; 149:1 and Isa. 42:10 issue the same invitation. Why new? Did it mean the old message wasn't adequate and constantly had to be revised? Or did it mean I constantly had to be singing new compositions and forgetting the old hymns, or even those songs composed yesterday? The invitations seem to occur when a new military victory has been experienced, although that is less evident in Psalm 98 than elsewhere. Each victory would understandably call for a new celebration. Alternatively, it has been suggested that it does mean that new songs were composed regularly for the great annual festivals. Whichever explanation is correct, it says to us that our worship should be fresh and not stale and tired. Whether we are celebrating new spiritual victories or recalling the old, old story, our worship should be vigorous, refreshed by our recent experiences of God's grace. If it isn't, give your worship a fresh injection by taking a little time to review God's specific mercies in your life and bring them to him in praise.

 ORIENTATION: The point of this psalm, as seen in the repeated commands of vv. 5 and 9, is an invitation to worship. As always, however, the worship is not to be a superficial emotion, but a well-grounded response to God, deeply informed by his character and his actions.

MAP: Praising the Lord involves:

Affirmation, 1–3
- The Lord is universal in his sovereignty.
- The Lord is majestic in his holiness.

Meditation, 4–5
- On the character of God, 4a, 5.
- On the experience of God, 4b, in Israel.

Illustration, 6–8
- He is a God who answers, 6–7.
- He is a God who acts, 8, in discipline and forgiveness.

Invitation, 5, 9
The invitation is both a solemn call to reverence, bowing low at his footstool, and a gracious call to draw near 'at his holy mountain'.

SIGNPOSTS: We were reminded yet again on our recent holiday how mountains inspire awe. Frequently shrouded in clouds, their solid grandeur and immense proportions evoke a sense of eternity and make us humans feel very small. No wonder they play such a significant part in Israel's story as places where God made himself known. This psalm invites us to 'worship at his holy mountain'. That, of course, was a way of inviting people to the temple in Jerusalem. The NT calls Christians also to worship at a mountain, but not the temple in Jerusalem. We are called to join a multitude of others as pilgrims to 'Mount Zion, to the city of the living God, the heavenly Jerusalem'. In contrast to the fearsome impression made by Sinai, ours is a mountain where angels and 'the firstborn' gather in 'joyful assembly' and celebrate the work of Jesus our mediator. Yet joy should never spill over into presumption and we still need to pay careful attention to God's voice from the mountain, 'for our "God is [still] a consuming fire"' (Heb. 12:29, quoting Deut. 4:24).

Psalm 100 ✓

 ORIENTATION: This short psalm brings the 'homage psalms' that began with Psalm 93 to a close.

 MAP: The psalm contains four commands.

Shout, 1

The whole earth is summoned to express jubilant praise.

Serve, 2

'Serve' is the word the RSV uses at the beginning of this verse. Worship is far more than the singing of songs. The whole of our lives must be offered in the service of God with gladness. See Rom. 12:1–2.

Know, 3

Informed worship is preferable to ignorant noise, especially when the information is based on experience. Here the truth is of God as our Maker and Shepherd (see 95:4–7).

Enter, 4–5

Worship is about drawing near and entering into God's presence, and not about speaking to God from a safe distance. Verse 5 explains why we can be bold. It is because 'his love endures for ever'. Hebrews develops the theme of entering God's presence.

SIGNPOST: Years ago, when Ceausescu was firmly in control in Romania, I walked though the streets of Bucharest and past the parliament building. Truth to tell, I kept my distance, as seemed only wise in view of the heavily armed soldiers guarding it. They didn't exactly look friendly. Soon after the revolution took place in 1989, I returned for the founding of the Evangelical Alliance in Romania. Guess where the meetings were held! The parliament building from which I and, more significantly, countless Romanian Christians had been excluded was now one we entered with confidence to celebrate God's salvation. There are so many buildings housing the centres of power or prestige on earth that we have no right to enter. But we have an invitation – and, thanks to the work of Christ, also a right – to enter God's very presence. Heb. 10:19–39 gives us the guidance we need to do so with a right combination of confidence and caution.

The beauty of the Psalms: Poetry

Psalms is a book of beauty and superb artistry. We can gain a deeper appreciation of it by knowing something of how its poetry 'works'. Inevitably much is lost in translation, such as the sound of words, alliterations and word play, and even rhythm and rhyme, but the essentials can still be seen. Hebrew poetry is characterized by a rhythm of sense rather than sound, but much rhythm is evident when good English translations are read.

The most obvious feature of Hebrew poetry, unlike traditional English poetry where rhythm and rhyme are the keys, is that of parallelism. It takes three forms. In synonymous parallelism, the second line repeats the thought of the first, as in 1:2. In antithetical parallelism the second line contrasts with the first, as in 1:6. In synthetic parallelism the second line develops the thought of the first, as in 37:3–4. Many psalms display a complex use of parallelism, such as 5:3–4 and the four lines of 30:5 which illustrate both antithetical and synthetic parallelism.

A reader is immediately struck by the sheer descriptive force of the psalms. Frequent use is made of metaphor and imagery, as when the psalms declare 'The Lord is my rock', or 'my strong tower', or 'my Shepherd'. Occasionally they use a simile, as when the first psalm says the righteous 'are like a tree planted by streams of water' and the wicked 'are like chaff'. Hebrew poetry is also marked by conciseness. Its economy of words extends to omitting obvious words, especially verbs, on occasions, as in 114:4.

Strophes and stanzas are used, but the most common structural features consist of the use of refrains (see 42:5, 11; 43:5) and acrostics. The most notable example of an acrostic poem is 119. Other examples can be found in 25, 34, 111, 112 and 145.

The Psalms encourage us to use the best artistic craftsmanship in our offering of worship. The beauty of the Psalms is not an end in itself, but a vehicle to lead us to God.

Psalm 101

 ORIENTATION: Here is a prayer that the psalmist might live 'a life of integrity' (v. 2, NLT) or 'a blameless life'. Integrity is essentially about integration, a lack of fragmentation.

MAP: The psalm points to a number of contrasting areas and causes me to ask, 'Am I consistent?'

Private and public

Verse 2 speaks of the affairs of the home and v. 8 of the affairs of the city.

Thought and action

Verse 3 first speaks of how the mind is fed (see Phil. 4:8) and then, together with v. 7, of how life is lived.

Individual and social

Throughout the psalm there is a very personal emphasis on 'I', which occurs twelve times. But vv. 5–7 deal with choosing companions carefully and recognize the importance of our social networks. See Prov. 13:20; 1 Cor. 15:33.

Will and emotion

The psalm is laced with evidence of the psalmist's determination in its frequent use of 'I will'. Yet it is also a song that recognizes the place of deep emotions in its references both to joy ('sing') and hate.

LINKS: Matt. 22:16 speaks of Jesus as 'a man of integrity'.

SIGNPOST: Integrity is a rare quality in today's world, but if others lack it, Christians are called to possess it. James's letter is about a life of integrity. Early on he signals a concern about the perils of 'double-mindedness' (1:8). Then, throughout his letter, he teaches that being a disciple involves being single-minded and wholehearted in following God. Disciples should remove 'all moral filth' from their lives and make space for God's word (1:21). They should put into practice what they hear (1:22), keeping the whole law, not just a part (2:8–11). Their deeds should match their claims to faith (2:14–26). Their tongues should not be forked (3:1–12). Wisdom should come from above, not below (3:13–18). Essentially, they should prize friendship with God and shun friendship with the world (4:4). Speech needs to be plainly honest, not ambiguously duplicitous (4:12). Do I live a coherent life, in which the belief and actions, outer and inner aspects, religious and secular facets of my life are one? Or do I lack integrity?

 ORIENTATION: While this is one of the seven penitential psalms (see Ps. 6), some say there are three poems here, joined together on the loose theme of time: passing time (vv. 1–11), appointed time (vv. 12–22) and enduring time (vv. 23–28). Each witnesses to God being in control of time. Certainly lament (vv. 1–11, 23–24) alternates with faith (vv. 12–22, 25–28).

MAP: The key lessons are:

Life is passing, 1–11

In a situation of particular difficulty, the psalmist realizes that:

- days 'vanish like smoke', 3;
- days perish 'like grass', 4, 11;
- days pass 'like the evening shadow', 11;
- days are fragile and uncertain, 23.

Time is planned, 12–22

Yet:

- God rules over time in heaven, 12;
- God has a plan in time for Jerusalem, 13–17;
- God has reserved future time for praise, 18–22.

God is permanent, 23–28

- He was, 24–25: 'In the beginning . . .'
- He is, 27: 'you remain the same';
- He is to come, 27b: 'your years will never end'.

SIGNPOST: Psalm 102:6–7 reminds me of the amazing ability of God's word to pierce a heart, like an arrow hitting its target. One night in London, Billy Graham used these verses as his text. At first sight it doesn't seem the most promising of texts for an evangelist, but he described the sense of loneliness the image provokes and the way some people experience life as a desolate wasteland. Dr Graham used the AV's translation: 'I am like a pelican of the wilderness. I am like an owl of the desert.' The actual bird is uncertain, although most agree now that the AV's pelican is really an owl! No matter. Dr Graham then pointed to the good news of Christ, who came to bring abundant life. The next day, Mrs Graham was visiting a London department store and met a sales assistant who had heard the sermon and said it described him exactly. As a result he came to Christ. Truly, 'the word of God is alive and active [even Ps. 102:6–7]. Sharper than any double-edged sword . . .' (Heb. 4:12–13)

My days . . . your years

Psalm 103 ✓ ▷

 ORIENTATION: This intricately woven poem is both expansive and inclusive. One of its favourite words is 'all', which occurs eight times in the TNIV's translation. It starts with the individual, but then develops its thought to embrace Israel until the whole of creation is involved.

MAP: The psalm addresses:

God and our forgetfulness, 1–5
In the light of our tendency to forget God, the psalm:
- issues the summons to remember, 1–2;
- details the substance to remember, 3–5: God forgives, heals, redeems, crowns, satisfies and renews.

God and our failings, 6–12
In the light of our tendency to sin, the psalm recalls:
- the character of God: just, revealing and merciful;
- the surprise of God, 10: 'he does not treat us as our sins deserve'.

God and our frailty, 13–18
In the light of our precarious lives, the psalm reflects on:
- the fatherhood of God, 13;
- the fragility of humans, 14–16;
- the security of God's love, 17–18.

God and our focus, 19–22
In the light of what has been said, the psalm ends with a renewed call to put God at the centre and to praise him.

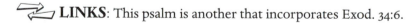 **LINKS**: This psalm is another that incorporates Exod. 34:6.

SIGNPOST: Study the eight 'alls' in this psalm, some of which are parallels. There is the 'all' of my worship, v. 1; the 'all' of God's benefits, v. 2; the 'all' of sins forgiven, v. 3; the 'all' of healing experienced, v. 3; the 'all' of God's concern, v. 6; the 'all' of God's rule, v. 19; the 'all' of creation's praise, vv. 21, 22. Is this too extravagant? Or, in the light of this, are our devotion and our discipleship sometimes too measured and restrained?

Psalm 104

 ORIENTATION: This celebration of the God of creation joins 8, 19 and 24 in seeing the earth, in all its wonder, as God's handiwork.

MAP: The psalm roughly follows the order of creation found in Gen. 1, though as a hymn it uses poetic licence and is not slavish in its obedience. It celebrates God's creation of:

The light of the heavens, 1–2, Gen. 1:3–5
The separation of the atmosphere, 3–4, Gen. 1:6–8
The boundaries of the water, 5–13, Gen. 1:9–10
The growth of vegetation, 14–18, Gen. 1:11–13
The passage of time, 19–23, Gen. 1:14–19
The creation of creatures, 24–26, Gen. 1:20–23
The formation of life, 27–30, Gen. 1:24–28; Acts 17:28
The provision of food, 27–28, Gen. 1:29–31
The praise of the Creator, 31–35, captured well by Robert Grant's hymn
'O Worship The King':

> O Lord of all might, how boundless thy love!
> While angels delight to hymn thee above,
> the humbler creation though feeble their lays,
> with true adoration shall sing to thy praise.

SIGNPOST: This is not an 'innocent' celebration of creation, but a polemical one with which non-Israelites would have disagreed profoundly. Other nations had different views of how the world was made and certainly did not accept that the Lord Yahweh had made the world out of nothing. Some of this psalm echoes Egyptian poetry, which ascribes creation to sun deities. Babylon thought Marduk manufactured the world from the body of his enemy Tiamat and made humans as slaves. Ancient accounts of creation contain mythical creatures fighting over chaos and the sun and moon were worshipped as independent powers. Here is an unapologetic assertion that one God, Yahweh, made the world from nothing and rules over all its heights and its depths, its stars and its creatures, its nature and its inhabitants. How we view creation affects how we treat it. God, who brought something out of nothing, light out of darkness and order out of chaos to create a good world, calls us to live responsibly on earth and care for the planet he made.

Clothed with splendour

Psalm 105 ✓

ORIENTATION: Sung when the ark was brought to Jerusalem (1 Chr. 16:8–36), the central part of this psalm retells the story of Israel from the call of Abraham to entry into the Promised Land. Its purpose is to convince people 'to follow his principles and obey his laws' (v. 45, NLT). It all leads to this final verse, but it provides an extraordinarily rich journey en route.

MAP: The following crumbs from this lengthy psalm might prove nourishing.

Seeking the Lord's strength, 4
- The need to focus on the Lord, not someone else.
- The need for urgency: 'keep on searching' (NLT).
- The need for help: vv. 1–5 suggest that worship and memory are important in finding the Lord's strength.
- The need for purpose: the reason for his strength is found in v. 45.

Believing the Lord's promise, 8
- The key principle is found in v. 8.
- Many illustrations are found in vv. 8–44.

Understanding the Lord's testing, 17
- Read the background in Gen. 39 – 40; NB Gen. 39:21.
- Think of the bewilderment Joseph must have felt.
- Understand the purpose, as God tests and moulds Joseph's character.

SIGNPOST: Until the Enlightenment, when history supposedly became an objective discipline, it was viewed as a storehouse of moral and spiritual lessons. That's certainly how Psalm 105 treats the story of Israel and also how the NT views the OT, at least in part. Paul writes, 'For everything that was written in the past was written to teach us, so that through the endurance taught in the Scriptures and the encouragement they provide we might have hope' (Rom. 15:4). The 'honour board' of faith in Heb. 11 is a perfect illustration of this. Have we grown too proud and think we can no longer learn from the past? Have we neglected the stories, especially from the OT, that can still prove to be wise teachers? If so, we are ignoring the wonderful resource God has given us for our Christian lives at our peril. Let's set about reading and learning from the stories of Israel.

Five books or one?

The average reader of the Psalms probably pays little attention to the fact that the whole book is composed of a collection of five shorter books. For them it is probably the individual psalms that matter. If thought is given to the question at all, it is probably concluded that the five books are meant to imitate the five books of Moses. But the Psalms as a whole was not haphazardly thrown together and there is evidence that thought has been given to its editing.

Book 1 consists of Psalms 1 – 41; Book 2 of Psalms 42 – 72; Book 3 of Psalms 73 – 89; Book 4 of Psalms 90 – 106 and Book 5 of 107 – 150. Each book concludes with a doxology, while Psalms 1 and 150 are clearly designed as a suitable introduction and conclusion for the whole work. Royal psalms are found at the 'seams' of the first three books (2, 72, 89).

According to Gerald Wilson, many of the royal psalms occur in Books 1–3. Psalm 2 introduces David's throne and Psalm 72 concerns his successors, but Psalm 89 speaks of the dynasty's collapse. Psalm 89 sets the scene for the latter books to deal with the downfall of David's dynasty and the spiritual crisis it provoked by emphasizing Yahweh as King and retelling the longer story of Israel. They encourage Israel to persevere in hope despite the exile.

Walter Brueggemann detects a movement from a stress on obedience in Books 1 and 2 to praise in Books 3–5, with Psalm 73 as a pivot. The tone certainly shifts from lament to praise at the end. Some see a comparable shift from an individual to a communal focus. It is Book 4 that contains the psalms that celebrate God as King (93 – 100) and Book 5 that contains the pilgrimage songs (120 – 136) and the Hallel praise psalms of 113 – 118 and 146 – 150. It ends on the positive note that, whatever happens to David's throne, God is still ruling the earth from his throne in heaven.

As Derek Kidner usefully summarizes it: 'The picture that emerges is a mixture of order and informality of arrangement, which invites but also defeats an attempt to account for every detail of its final form.'

Psalm 106 ✓

ORIENTATION: This and Psalm 105 are 'non-identical twins' (Wilcock). The previous psalm dwelt on the value of memory; this one does the reverse and emphasizes the danger of forgetting. See, e.g., vv. 13 and 21.

MAP: The following gives us our bearings in this long psalm.

The call to remember, 1–5

Although the message of the psalm concerns the way Israel forgot God, here, ironically, the poet offers praise and asks God to remember him.

The confession of failure, 6–46

The central section of the psalm recalls Israel's tragic history from the exodus to settlement in Canaan. The belief they exhibited at the Red Sea, mentioned in v. 12, soon gave way to the amnesia of the desert, mentioned in the very next verse. Verses 13–15 are a microcosm of the wider story:

- they forgot God's acts, 13a;
- they ignored God's word, 13b;
- they tested God's patience, 14;
- they encountered God's anger, 15.

The consolation of memory, 44–46

While Israel forgot, God 'remembered his covenant' and showed them mercy.

The cry for salvation, 47–48

Now scattered among the nations, Israel need saving again, for their spiritual amnesia has led them into further trouble.

SIGNPOST: First impressions can be misleading. Each item in this lengthy catalogue of Israel's failure takes us back to an earlier OT story. Let's look at just one. When we first meet Phinehas (mentioned in v. 30) in Num. 25, he seems to be a zealous young man who delights in killing an Israelite man and his Midianite woman whose relationship compromised Israel. He is jealous for God's honour and his action stemmed God's anger and saved Israel from further judgment. Our next sight of him, in Num. 31:6, shows him leading Israel into battle. But in Josh. 22 (it's worth reading!) we get an altogether different picture. When a conflict arose among the tribes of Israel, Phinehas exercises great wisdom and diplomacy, calms it down and brings about reconciliation. Based on his previous record, he wouldn't have been my first choice as a diplomat, but first impressions can be wrong. A balanced man, Phinehas is – concerned for the purity, victory and unity of God's people. Not a bad model, after all.

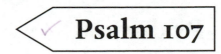

 ORIENTATION: Kidner writes, 'The centre-piece of this striking psalm is the set of four word-pictures of human predicaments and divine interventions.' Indeed, this wonderfully composed psalm testifies to God's amazing ability to transform the worst of situations.

MAP: The psalm contains:

Gratitude for redemption, 1–3
- gratitude is invited, 1;
- gratitude should be expressed, 2–3.

Litany of redemption, 4–32
Four situations of human extremity are described:
- lost travellers are given guidance and provision, 4–9;
- despairing prisoners are given freedom and light, 10–15;
- terminal sufferers are given healing and hope, 16–22;
- storm-tossed sailors are given peace and safety, 22–32.

Reflections on redemption, 33–43
Ranging away from the individual situations, the psalm invites the wise to 'ponder the loving deeds of the Lord' (v. 43) more widely. Then they would see his transformation:
- of the barren wilderness, 33–38;
- of many barren lives, 39–43.

SIGNPOST: Redemption – one of the big words of the Christian faith – means to secure someone's liberty from captivity, usually by paying a price. In the OT God releases the children of Israel from Egypt at the cost of the lives of the Egyptian firstborn. All Israel's firstborn belong to God, but are redeemed in other ways. It was the word for the release of slaves. Ruth is set free from hard times by the kinsman-redeemer. This strict meaning of redemption is broadened in this psalm to include people being rescued from dangerous situations. Christ is our Redeemer who, at the cost of his own life, sets us free from captivity to law, sin and Satan. 'In him we have redemption through his blood, the forgiveness of sins, in accordance with the riches of God's grace' (Eph. 1:7). When we have good news of someone being set free, we have no problem sharing it with others. So, as this psalm says, 'Let the redeemed of the Lord' tell their story.

Psalm 108

ORIENTATION: This psalm is unusual as one of three psalms of David in Book 5. It is a combination of two others. The opening verses come from 57:7–11 and these are joined from v. 6 onwards by verses from 60:5–12. Psalm 60 began on a despairing note and emphasized the feeling of rejection, but this psalm, with its different beginning, is much more positive. The opening words summon a struggling believer to focus on God. The words 'My heart, O God, is steadfast' speak of the psalmist's determination to trust and go on believing even when his circumstances tell him it is foolish to do so. Sometimes, when circumstances are grim, holding on to faith is all that you can do.

 MAP: The psalm is composed of three movements.

Determination in the light of God's love, 1–5
Confident of God's love (4–5), the psalmist refuses to give up on God (1) and makes a very public noise about his faith (2–3).

Supplication in the light of God's word, 6–9
Confident of God's word (7), the psalmist pleads for God's deliverance (6), knowing he has kept his promise to Israel before (8–9).

Anticipation in the light of God's power, 10–13
Confident of God's power (12–13), the mood changes and the psalmist envisages being led into the city again in victory (10–11).

SIGNPOST: 'Steadfast' is a great, if dated, word. It speaks of fixedness, determination, resolve, steadiness, constancy, perseverance and unshakability. In the recent Olympic Games the commentators spoke several times of the way gold medallists had gained their victories after defeat four years previously or despite major setbacks and injuries. Their steadfastness was the key. It bred strength. In our fast-paced world of flat-pack everything where nothing lasts for long, this is a rare quality. People's lives are a series of disconnected chapters without any necessary thread between them. Unless a project yields instant success, it is usually abandoned. Values are as changeable as the weather, beliefs discarded as easily as yesterday's clothes. Discouragements knock previously held certainties. But true success comes from steadfastness, in spiritual as well as sporting matters.

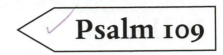

Psalm 109

 ORIENTATION: This third psalm of David in quick succession is the most powerful and vitriolic of the psalms of vengeance. Striking a very different note from most of Book 5, it is a throwback to some psalms found earlier in the collection. It may be the editor's way of reminding readers of the problems of Davidic kingship and laying a path to celebrating God's kingship.

MAP: Through the rage, the following logic is apparent:

The complaint he voices, 1–5

He suffers unjustified (3) and unexpected (4) attack.

The justice he seeks, 6–15

As if in a law court, he seeks:

- a guilty verdict, 6–7;
- an exemplary sentence, 8–13;
- an unending punishment, 14–15.

The case he makes, 16–20

- he has suffered power abuse, 16;
- he has suffered verbal abuse, 17–19;
- he seeks the abuse to rebound on them, 20.

The judge he trusts, 21–31

The judge dispenses:

- powerful love, 21: 'Sovereign Lord';
- righteous love, 22–25;
- saving love, 26–31.

SIGNPOST: So far we have tried to understand the psalms of vengeance chiefly in their OT context. Their antagonism towards evil and their desire that God should mete out judgment suggest that there may still be room for them in our worship. There is a place for righteous anger. But there's no justification for the harmful expression of personal anger, or for feeding a quest for revenge. Shortly after writing, 'In your anger do not sin', Paul writes, 'Get rid of all bitterness, rage and anger . . . Be kind and compassionate to one another' (Eph. 4:26, 31–32). Those of a passionate disposition may find this difficult, but personality is no excuse. The secret of personal transformation is simple, yet demanding. We use our wills to put off the old self and put on the new. We can't do this unless the Holy Spirit helps us by renewing our minds, changing our attitudes, focus, desires and values, and enabling us to be more God-like (see Eph. 4:20 – 5:1).

Psalm 110

 ORIENTATION: The title claims that David authored this psalm. Verse 1 speaks of God's ('The Lord') promise to his earthly king ('my lord'). Some think of it as a coronation anthem. The picture given of an ideal kingship exceeds what any ordinary human ruler could expect. The psalm points to the reign of God himself, an increasing focus at the end of the Psalms, and to a coming Messiah.

MAP: God is the principal actor throughout. The use of 'the Lord' (*Yahweh*), the personal name of God, in vv. 1, 2 and 4, and 'Lord' (*adonai*), a reference to God as Master, in v. 5 gives a fourfold structure to the psalm.

The Lord says: the king is appointed, 1
The king ascends the throne at God's invitation and decree. God takes the initiative and guarantees a victorious outcome.

The Lord wills: the king is aided, 2–3
God promises to extend the king's rule and territory, providing troops who are ready and equipped for battle.

The Lord has: the king is assured, 4
An irrevocable oath is given. A new idea is introduced that the king is also a priest from the order of Melchizedek, who was the king of Salem. Gen. 14:18 provides the background to this. In this way, the king is introduced as a king of peace.

The Lord is: the king is victorious, 5–7
Victory belongs to the Lord God, who supports the king by being at his right hand, until all his enemies are finally defeated.

SIGNPOST: This is the most frequently cited psalm in the NT, mentioned some thirty times. By Jesus' day, and with the failure of the Davidic line of kings, it was thought to refer to the coming Messiah whose kingdom would never end. In Mark 12:35–37 Jesus points out that David speaks in the psalm of the Messiah as 'my Lord' and so greater than he was. The early Christians readily identified this Messiah with Jesus of Nazareth, as demonstrated in Acts 2:34 and Heb. 1:13; 5:6; 7:17, 21; 10:12, 13. The psalm therefore presents Jesus Christ as universal King (vv. 1–3) and eternal Priest (v. 4) and, Kidner adds, victorious Warrior (vv. 5–7).

Who wrote the Psalms?

There are various opinions about the value of the titles attached to the psalms. Some think them original, while others think they were added much later and so consider them unreliable. But there is no real reason for uncertainty. The psalms fit the claims made in the titles perfectly. Three names frequently occur in connection with collections of psalms that have been included.

David is the best known of these. The shepherd-king, whose story is told extensively in 1 Sam. 16 – 2 Sam. 24, was also a musician and poet. His psalms mostly come towards the beginning of the book, with 51 – 65 forming a particular group, and mirror the ups and downs of his public and family life. They chart his time on the run from Saul, the hopes and aspirations of his throne, the bringing of the ark to Jerusalem, his many battles, his sin with Bathsheba and the tragedy of Absalom's rebellion. Their poetry vividly captures the experience of these events and proves a wonderful vehicle for the expression of the strong emotions involved.

Asaph's collection of psalms is included as 50, 73 – 83. A passage in 1 Chronicles tells us he was a worship leader who headed up a musical guild in the temple. He is mentioned in 1 Chr. 6:39; 15:17, 19; 25:2, 6 and 2 Chr. 5:12. He was 'the master of music' when the ark of the covenant was brought into Jerusalem (1 Chr. 16:4–6). His compositions involve both praise and lament, reflecting the fluctuating fortunes of Israel, but particularly dwell on what they felt to be God's rejection of Israel. The pivotal Psalm 73 is one of his compositions.

The other collection comes from 'the sons of Korah'. Scattered a little through the first three books of Psalms, they are found in 42 – 49; 84 – 85; 87 – 88. These Levites (1 Chr. 6:16; 9:19) served in the temple and were identified with the Kohathite music guild (1 Chr. 6:33) who led worship through several generations. It is difficult to relate their psalms to any particular events, but they show a strong focus on Jerusalem and God's kingship. The name of Korah was infamous in Israel's history (see Num. 16) and their prominence in the Psalms is a marvellous testimony to a name and family finding redemption.

Hallelujah!

🧭 **ORIENTATION**: Psalms 111 – 113 all begin with the single word 'Hallelujah!' (or 'Praise the Lord' in several English translations). This personal hymn of praise is an acrostic with each of its twenty-two lines starting with a new letter. Its subject matter – the works of the Lord – makes it closely related to the following psalm. This psalm is striking for the way the adjectives describing God's work are paired.

🗺 **MAP**: The psalmist rejoices in:

God's works, 3: 'glorious and majestic';

God's nature, 4: 'gracious and compassionate';

God's activities, 7: 'faithful and just';

God's words, 8: 'faithfulness and uprightness';

God's blessing, 9: 'holy and awesome'.

🪧 **SIGNPOST**: The psalmists frequently used an acrostic form as a means of structuring their songs. Perhaps it was also a device to help them memorize their words. It's easy enough for even well-known performers to forget their words (I could name names, but won't) and every aid helps. It's a very simple design in which each line (or verse) begins with a different letter of the alphabet in order. Why not compose your own acrostic of praise? It might start something like this: **A**wesome are the works of the Lord; his **B**lessings come in abundance, and his **C**ompassion never fails towards me. **D**eliverance from sin is now mine, and **E**very day I know his mercies anew. The **F**ellowship of God's people supports me and the **G**oodness of God is my experience in a land of evil . . . Have a go: I'm sure yours will be better than mine!

ORIENTATION: This psalm rejoices in a godly family and speaks of the resulting blessings of a good life which overflows in blessing to those outside the family and the next generation.

MAP: A guide to the good life involves the following topics:

Identity, 1

The good life is forged by being centred on God. Note the unusual balance of 'fear' and 'delight' in this verse.

Legacy, 2–3

Those who live the good life leave a rich legacy in their children and in their impact on others, through both their riches and their righteousness.

Generosity, 4–5, 9

The good life is marked by a generosity of spirit, seen in the use of words such as 'gracious and compassionate', and generosity with wealth, as such people lend 'freely' and 'scatter abroad' their gifts.

Integrity, 5

Characterized by 'righteousness', those who live the good life conduct their affairs 'with justice'.

Stability, 6–8

Even when facing bad news or dreadful circumstances, the hearts of such people are 'secure' because of their trust in God.

The concluding verse speaks of the effect of the righteous on the wicked, who will react with envy and descend into a void.

SIGNPOST: Here is a picture of 'the good life'. It doesn't consist of sand, sun and sangria, as many foolishly believe, but of a happy family whose reputation is respected and whose name is honoured in the community. Their secret is that they 'fear the Lord'. Many Christian families can testify to God's blessing in terms similar to this psalm. Do we celebrate it, as the psalm does? Or, in view of the tragic breakdown of family life and the fear of hurting others' feelings, do we keep quiet about it? We should never boast in ourselves or be insensitive to the struggles many face, but it's wrong not to be thankful for the gift of God's blessing in family life, often through several generations. Too often we dwell on the negative. Emphasizing the positive means we can encourage people to better things rather than accepting the worst. There are no guarantees, but a good family life starts when people fear the Lord.

Psalm 113 ✓

 ORIENTATION: Psalm 113 is the last in the trio of praise psalms, but the first of the *Hallel* psalms (113 – 118) that were sung at the Passover.

MAP: This psalm captures two great truths about God that we would ordinarily regard as being in contradiction to each other.

God sits enthroned, 1–5

God is worthy of praise because of:
- his eternal character, 2: 'now and for evermore';
- his global reach, 3–4: 'from the rising of the sun';
- his supreme position, 4: 'above the heavens';
- his unique nature, 5: 'who is like . . . ?'

God stoops down, 6–9

His awesome nature and position do not make him indifferent to our needs or immune from our struggles. He not only sees our situation, but also transforms it. Two illustrations of his gracious condescension are given. They are:
- to the poor on the scrapheap, 7–8;
- to the childless woman in her loneliness, 9.

SIGNPOST: Jesus would have sung these words on the night of the Last Supper (Matt. 26:30), for the first two *Hallel* psalms were sung before the Passover meal and the last four at its conclusion. Its theme of God using his power to help the downtrodden makes it a suitable prelude to the following psalms where the exodus theme becomes more prominent. But try entering into the mind of Christ as he sang this psalm on that fatal night, knowing what was to follow. Would 'the One who sits enthroned on high' (v. 5) stoop down to rescue him, as he prayed in Gethsemane? The answer was a firm 'No'. The refusal was not because God was unable to do so, but because a greater plan was in operation. This incomparable God (vv. 4–5) works in unusual ways. He refused to exercise his power and deliver his firstborn Son *from* death. He chose rather to deliver his Son *to* death, and so make a new exodus possible, for people from all nations, as the tyranny of sin and Satan was broken. So today the poor and needy around the world can sing this psalm with a new depth, for the Son of God stooped down to the cross.

ORIENTATION: Some events are so momentous that they can be described only as earth-shaking or earth-shattering. So it was with the exodus and Israel's entry into the Promised Land. Brueggemann describes the exodus as a 'world-transforming memory', which we are all invited to recall actively.

MAP: The mention of Jacob, in vv. 1 and 7, provides a frame for this psalm.

The family of Jacob, 1–2

They were:

- founded on God's deliverance, 1a: 'out of Egypt';
- formed around God's presence, 2a: 'God's sanctuary';
- forged by God's rule, 2b: 'his dominion'.

The miracle of Jacob, 3–6

To become a people in their own land, Israel had to overcome a series of obstacles – the Red Sea, the Sinai Desert and the River Jordan – which they did in each case miraculously. Regarding those barriers, these verses contain:

- a statement of what happened, 3–4;
- a question about why it happened, 5–6.

The God of Jacob, 7–8

These verses speak of:

- his awesome presence;
- his transforming power.

SIGNPOST: Boxing Day 2004 was unforgettable. That day the tsunami hit the many shores of India, Sri Lanka, Thailand and the Philippines. For those of us watching on the television it was awesome, but for those who were there it was terrifying. Survivors would have the memory etched in their minds for ever. The first signal of the approaching terror was that the waters fled. Centuries before, in another awesome event that occurred in nature, 'the sea looked and fled' (v. 3). To the Egyptian soldiers pursuing the fleeing Israelites, it spelled disaster. To the Israelites themselves, it spelled salvation as they crossed over the Red Sea on dry ground to safety (see Exod. 14:31). You don't forget an experience like that! It was etched deep into the memory of the whole nation. Israel could see it wasn't the forces of nature but the hand of God at work for their benefit. It showed them what God was like: a God of power and salvation. No wonder they invite the earth to 'tremble . . . at the presence of the Lord' (v. 7).

Psalm 115 ✓

 ORIENTATION: The simple yet arresting words of the first verse tell us that God alone is worthy of praise. The rest of the psalm tells us why.

MAP: We can praise him by comparison (vv. 2–8), through confession (vv. 9–11), with confidence (vv. 12–15) and in contemplation (vv. 16–18). Another framework might suggest we have a God for all the phases of our lives:

Eternal God, 1–8: living and reigning from the beginning.

Present God, 9–11: a help and shield today.

Future God, 12–15: who will bless our family's future.

Everlasting God, 16–18: who receives praise from the living.
Yet again, the key to the psalm might be the character of God himself:

Living God, 2–8: in contrast to idols.

Gracious God, 9–11: who is our help and shield.

Giving God, 12–15: who gives blessing and fruitfulness.

Eternal God, 16–18: the God of the highest heavens now and for evermore.

SIGNPOST: Three common but erroneous views of God are ruled out in this psalm. First, it rules out pantheism, or its variation, panentheism. This teaches that God has no separate existence, but is everywhere or in everything. It is a common feature of Eastern religions. But this psalm claims that 'our God is in heaven' (v. 3) and thereby stresses not his spatial distance from earth, but his transcendence over his creation and his difference and separateness from it. Second, it rules out polytheism. This teaches that there are many gods of a roughly equivalent kind, a view much beloved by secular politicians. This psalm rejects that, saying that God rules supreme over all from heaven and can easily be distinguished from the idols and petty deities that humans manufacture on earth (vv. 4–8). He is unique, not one among many. Third, it rules out deism. This teaches that God made the world, but then set it off on its own and is no longer involved. When v. 16 says 'the earth he has given to humankind', it doesn't mean that God is an absent deity. It is evident from the rest of the psalm that he isn't! It means that he has given the earth to human beings as a gift, but also as a responsibility.

'Make music to the Lord'

The psalms are above all songs to be sung by the people of God in worship rather than poems to be read or chanted. Fifty-five psalms are addressed to 'the director of music' (see the titles of 4; 5; 6; 8; 9, etc.) and almost two-thirds have some musical reference in their title, even if their meaning may now be somewhat obscure. They often exhort people to make music to the Lord (33:2; 57:7; 68:4; 81:2; 92:1; 98:4–6; 147:7; 149:3, etc.). Psalm 68:24–27 reports a musical procession to the temple where singers and musicians lead a vast throng to God. About twenty musical instruments are mentioned in all. Psalm 150 lists some, but also gives insight into the sense of exuberant joy they expressed.

The prominence of music in David's and Solomon's court is evident from 1 and 2 Chronicles. Numerous musicians are mentioned by name in 1 Chr. 6, while 1 Chr. 25:7 mentions that there were 288 of them. They were organized into guilds and served by rotation. The Chronicles reveal three important things. First, music was seen as 'ministry' in the presence of God. It wasn't secular art, a means of self-expression or a demonstration of professional competence, but service to God and his people. Second, since they were doing it for the Lord, 'they were trained and skilled' in their music. The worship of God demanded the highest standards. Third, music was both inclusive and levelling, for 'young and old alike, teacher as well as student, cast lots for their duties'.

The Psalms acknowledge the power of music both to express emotions and to alter them. Many laments begin in a minor key expressing despair, but then transpose into a major key of praise. As 45:8 claims, 'the music of the strings makes you glad'. But music also transports people beyond themselves and the Psalms picture humans as being caught up with the music of the whole of creation in praise of God (see 65:12–13; 96:11–13; 98:7–9; 103:22).

Music seems intrinsic to human nature and so should be a fundamental medium by which we express our relationship with God, using the best possible artistry in doing so, as is worthy of him.

Psalm 116 ✓

⊛ **ORIENTATION**: The underlying note of this thanksgiving psalm is the way the Lord values those he loves. It surfaces in v. 15. The psalm arises from another desperate, if unspecified, situation in which God rescues his loved ones.

🗺 **MAP**: The psalm is usually divided into three parts: 1–7, 8–14 and 15–19, each of which mentions death and ends with a commitment to action. But it can be viewed this way: after the initial setting-out of the psalmist's cry for help in vv. 1–4, the psalm splits into two parts detailing what the psalmist has received and what he has given.

What I received from the Lord, 4–11

- answered prayer, 4–5, 10–11;
- effective protection, 6–8;
- continuous presence, 9: 'I walk in the Lord's presence as I live here on earth' (NLT).

What I offered to the Lord, 12–19

Verse 12 is the pivot, indicating a move from reception to giving, not as a payment to God for services rendered, but as a free act of thanksgiving. Three elements interweave:

- the sacrifice of praise;
- the fulfilment of promises;
- the renewal of service.

✝ **SIGNPOST**: An elderly member of our church was dying in hospital. Some eager deacons were encouraging the church to pray fervently for her recovery and return home, where she lived alone. They were somewhat shocked when I asked them why they felt we should pray like this. She loved the Lord and had enjoyed a long life, her affairs were in order and she was ready to go to her eternal home. Did they not believe that to be with the Lord was a better option (Phil. 1:23)? Their praying was not really informed by Christian truth. The words 'Precious in the sight of the Lord is the death of those faithful to him' (v. 15) probably originally meant, according to the context, that delivering a faithful believer from death was costly ('precious' in that sense) to God. But since the resurrection of Christ, we may take it in the more obvious way: the death of believers is highly valued by God, for it brings them into his unbroken presence for ever.

Psalm 117

 ORIENTATION: Sung at the Passover meal, this psalm looks forward to God's universal rule. At first sight, this, the briefest of the psalms, is too short to say much about, but every phrase counts towards its great theme.

MAP: The psalm is patterned on several basic questions.

What? 'Praise the Lord'
The exhortation to 'praise the Lord' comes at the beginning and the end, like the bread in a sandwich. This straightforward exhortation is needed because we and others easily become spiritually lethargic or distracted, even though our creation purpose is to glorify God.

Who? 'All you nations'
The exhortation is not just to individuals, nor even to Israel, nor even to Christians. It's addressed to the nations, for God's creative and saving sovereignty is a global one. So Iraq, Indonesia, India, China, Peru, Russia and Nigeria are called upon to praise God as much as Britain, Spain and America. But how will the nations do this unless they hear the gospel? The words of Rom. 10:12–17 tell us.

Why? 'For . . . '
This is anything but an empty exhortation to praise. What is called for is a reasoned and well-founded response to God because of his *hesed* – his unfailing, covenant love and enduring faithfulness.

SIGNPOST: We're apt to laugh at people who claim they are going to build great business empires when all they've got is a little market stall, but that's how Marks and Spencer began! Sometimes dreams become realities. This little psalm, composed in a tiny and, to most eyes, insignificant nation, has a bold vision. All nations, all peoples are summoned to praise their God. It's the same with the church. Small and insignificant to most people (1 Cor. 1:26), it has a grand vision of its gospel growing 'all over the world' (Col. 1:6) and of its Lord being the means of mending our broken world and of reconciling it to its Maker (Col. 1:20–22). In its history, the church grew from a small bunch of backwater fishermen to conquer Rome and bring other empires to their knees. Is the audacious vision really so improbable? Those who belong to a shrinking church need have no fear. We must keep the vision of Psalm 117 alive.

Psalm 118 ✓

ORIENTATION: The last of the *Hallel* psalms (113 – 118) that were sung at the Passover meal: here a pilgrim on the way to the temple encourages his fellow travellers forward by singing of God's love.

MAP: The psalm reveals various dimensions of God's love.

Responsive love, 4–7
'I cried . . . The Lord is with me . . . '
Superior love, 8–9
It is better than trusting in human love and support.
Victorious love, 10–16
From feeling surrounded by enemies, he experiences the Lord's salvation. Note in v. 14 that the Lord is his strength, song and salvation.
Disciplined love, 17–21
The psalmist has been disciplined by the Lord, whose love does not come cheap. There is a stress here on the need to be righteous.
Transforming love, 22–24
What others write off as worthless, love transforms.
Celebrated love, 25–29

LINKS: The New Testament quotes vv. 22–23 in Matt. 21:44; Mark 12:10–11; Acts 4:11 and 1 Pet. 2:6–9.

SIGNPOST: The Passover was one of the three feasts of Israel for which pilgrims were expected to travel from all over the land to Jerusalem. It rehearsed the historical events of the exodus from Egypt and celebrated them as strong facts. But its repetition year after year had its dangers. It could become a cold history lesson, an institutionalized ritual or simply over-familiar. So in later Judaism the practice developed of reading the Song of Songs during the Passover. There is little direct connection between the Song and the Passover (see Song 1:9), but they used it as an allegory of God's dealing with them. It injected tones of personal intimacy, warm affection and wild celebration that woke Israel up and saved the Passover from the dangers inherent in it. God set them free because he loved them and they in return loved him with every fibre of their being. Read the Song of Songs for yourself and use it to celebrate not only the gift of human sexuality, but the love there is between yourself and God – a love 'as strong as death' (Song 8:6).

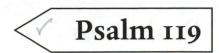

ORIENTATION: The running theme of this rich, lengthy acrostic poem is delight in God's law. Eight words are used interchangeably 'like a ring of eight bells' (Kidner) for God's word. In order of appearance they are 'law', meaning teaching or instruction (25 times), 'statutes' (23 times), 'precepts' (21 times), 'decrees' (22 times), 'commands' (14 times), 'laws', meaning judgment or regulations (20 times), 'word' (25 times) and 'promise' (11 times). Although concerned about sin (see vv. 11 and 133), it is essentially a positive psalm that celebrates the constructive role God's word plays in helping us negotiate the path of life (see vv. 32, 35, 101, 104, 105 and 128).

MAP: It is impossible to chart such a lengthy psalm in a few headings. Here attention is drawn to some key verses that speak of the value of God's word.
It protects the tempted, 9
It refreshes the weary, 25
It liberates the heart, 32, 45
It surpasses the material, 72, 127
It instructs the ignorant, 99
It flavours the commonplace, 103
It guides the perplexed, 105, 130
It stirs the emotions, 120, 161

SIGNPOST: Recent press reports tell us there are 1,043 laws in the UK that give inspectors the right to enter our homes. They include the right 'to inspect pot plants for pests, to measure the height of hedges, to search bedrooms for asylum seekers and to look at fridges for their energy rating' (*Daily Telegraph*, 21 July 2008). Half of them are new in the last decade and they are only a fraction of the total number of laws that parliament has passed in that time. No wonder we find laws burdensome and restrictive. Psalm 119 shows an altogether different attitude to law, which is wholly positive. It is a 'delight' (vv. 70, 77, 174), containing many wonderful things (v. 18), teaches good judgment (v. 66) and brings freedom (v. 45; see Jas 2:12) and peace (v. 165). Good law is like that: good laws on the road do not restrict freedom but, rather, by bringing order to a dangerous situation, bring safety and preserve life. Go through Psalm 119 noting the references to law and use this comprehensive picture to check your own attitude to God's law.

Psalm 120

On being a nonconformist

ORIENTATION: Psalms 120 – 134 are known as the 'songs of ascents' which accompanied the journeys of the pilgrims as they went up to Jerusalem. This one seems more personal than the others and describes the pilgrim's longing to get out of his situation where he is surrounded by lies, deceit and violence. He says, in effect, 'I don't belong here.'

Metaphorically, the psalmist is located in Meshek, in the far north, distant from Jerusalem, and in Kedar, which was in the south-east and populated by Arabs. These places, so far apart, are chosen for their symbolism rather than because they are his real habitations. They signify a godly Israelite being forced to live in inhospitable pagan or Gentile areas, away from God's presence in Jerusalem.

MAP: The key aspects are:

The cry for God's help, 1–2

The threat of God's punishment, 3–4

The longing for God's presence, 6–7

LINKS: It reminds us of the significance of the company we keep. Prov. 13:20 says, 'Walk with the wise and become wise,' and 1 Cor. 15:33 points out that 'bad company corrupts good character'.

SIGNPOST: In January 1992, 30,000 plastic ducks were swept off a container ship into the middle of the Pacific Ocean during a storm. They went where the currents took them. Two-thirds floated south to Indonesia, Australia and South America; 10,000 headed north, through the Bering Strait, across the Arctic Ocean and around America's Atlantic shore, and were heading for Britain fifteen years later! As Christians we shouldn't be plastic ducks, carried wherever the currents take us. Like the psalmist, Christians are constitutionally nonconformists, whatever their church affiliation. We don't 'go with the flow' and will never be fully at ease in a fallen world. We seek to live God's way and stand up for his agenda, while others pursue their own very different lifestyles and objectives. God loves nonconformists! Think of Noah, Gideon, Jeremiah, Daniel or . . . Jesus. Never be afraid to be a nonconformist. It's your birthright.

The Psalms and festivals

Hovering in the background of the Psalms were the great festivals of Israel. Although many psalms were used for regular and personal devotions, some of them were evidently composed for the great festival occasions and corporate acts of worship. Descriptions in 1 Chr. 6:31–32; 16:1–38 and 25:1–8 give us a picture of Israel's worship in which the Psalms would have been a prime ingredient.

The children of Israel were encouraged to make a pilgrimage to Jerusalem three times a year for the festivals of Passover (March–April time), Pentecost, or Weeks (May–June time), and Tabernacles (September–October time). Although there can be no precision, Psalms 113 – 118 are associated with the Passover; 29 and 68 with Pentecost and 68, 81, 92 – 96 and 120 – 134 with Tabernacles. The placing of 119 (with its emphasis on the law) between the two great collections of festival songs is significant for underlining the importance of the law.

Psalms such as 24 and 47 provided processional music. Psalm 110 is thought to have been composed for a coronation and 96 (and possibly 68) for the entry of the ark of the covenant into Jerusalem. Psalm 65 is clearly based on a festival, but which one is uncertain.

In the past scholars have suggested that a number of psalms related to an annual New Year festival when God was re-enthroned by his people, akin to festivals we know elsewhere. Mowinckel, the originator of this theory, based it especially on 93 – 99. A less extreme version of this view spoke about the place of the Psalms in an annual covenant renewal ceremony. But there is no hard evidence to support these theories which, at most, were supported by reading a predetermined interpretation into the text.

How should we use it in our worship today? Kidner suggests that the book of Psalms is not a library, storing up 'standard literature' for liturgical use, but 'a hospitable house, well lived in where most things can be found and borrowed after some searching', and whose first occupants have left the imprint of themselves on it. We can appropriate them, but need to make them our own.

Psalm 121

ORIENTATION: It is clear to see why pilgrims sang this song en route to Jerusalem, and why it's a favourite with many today. The opening sentence can be taken in two ways. Are the mountains a symbol of God's strength and a reference to his dwelling place – perhaps Mount Zion? If so, they point to the pilgrims' source of help. Or are they the location of the high places where other gods were worshipped? If so, the psalmist's point is that there is no help to be found there, but rather that the living Lord alone is the true source of help.

 MAP: Taken the second way, we see that:

God's help inspires confidence, 1–2
- The mountains are the high places of idol worship. They offer no help.
- The Lord alone is the true source of help.

God's watchfulness displays constancy, 3–4
- He gives his people acute attention, 3a.
- He gives his people constant attention, 3b–4.

God's protection proves comprehensive, 5–8
His thorough and unwavering protection covers:
- day and night;
- sun and moon (were they considered to have spiritual power?);
- coming and going;
- now and for ever.

SIGNPOST: Zygmunt Bauman has suggested that whereas the key symbol of people in previous generations was the pilgrim, today it's the tourist. Both are on journeys, passing through other people's territory, but there the similarity ends. Pilgrims are purposeful and travel in a group to which they belong, towards a spiritual destination. They journey in a morally responsible way and transform the places they pass through for the better (see 84:6). The journey may take them through inhospitable terrain at personal cost. By contrast, says Bauman, tourists are rich tramps. They've time to fill and are going nowhere in particular. They owe no loyalty to their fellow travellers and they take no responsibility for the territory they visit. They only leave litter behind for others to remove. Since they can pay, they expect others to serve them. And when one journey is over, they look forward to the next. Are we pilgrims or spiritual tourists?

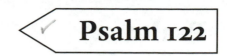

ORIENTATION: This second pilgrim psalm pictures pilgrims having arrived in Jerusalem. The wonderful note of joy in this psalm is not because of politics, but because of what the city represents.

MAP: Entering Jerusalem draws out:

Rejoicing in Jerusalem, 1–5
Because it is a place of:

- God's presence, 1;
- pilgrimage, 2, 4;
- protection, 3;
- power, 5.

Praying for Jerusalem, 6–9
Pray for:

- its peace;
- its prosperity (not material, but positive well-being).

LINKS: See Psalm 87.

SIGNPOST: Christians should pray for the peace of Jerusalem. We do not pray because we have a continuing spiritual need for the city: 'For here we do not have an enduring city, but we are looking for the city that is to come' (Heb. 13:14). We belong to 'the new Jerusalem' that will come 'down out of heaven from God' (Rev. 21:2). But we do pray out of respect for its strategic place in the story of God's salvation. We also pray because of its current pivotal place in the affairs of our world. No city has been or continues to be fought over so much and no city needs more prayer than this one. International peace depends greatly on what happens in the city of Jerusalem today, while peace with God depends entirely on what happened in the city of Jerusalem in Jesus' day. Jerusalem is a city that still needs our prayers.

Till he shows mercy

 ORIENTATION: Eugene Peterson rightly identifies the theme of this song of ascent as that of service. The circumstances may be less than ideal, as vv. 3–4 state, but our duty is still to serve God wholeheartedly.

 MAP: The psalm yields to the asking of simple questions.

What? 1a

'I lift up my eyes to you . . .' Our eyes easily roam. They need to be focused upwards on God, not on ourselves or even on our situation.

Where? 1b

'. . . who sit enthroned in heaven.' God reigns above and beyond all circumstances.

How? 2

As slaves to a master, as a servant woman to her mistress. That means we must serve God, not that he must serve us, and we should do so:

- attentively: the eyes need to be fixed on the needs and will of the master / mistress;
- patiently, waiting for their timing: 'till he shows . . . mercy';
- obediently: as any servant must do.

Why? 3–4

Because:

- we are in need;
- and God is a God of mercy.

SIGNPOST: I am not trying to be irreverent, but this psalm reminds me of taking a friend's small dog for a walk. The dog was full of beans and far too energetic for us lethargic human beings who had recently benefited from a good Sunday lunch, so he kept bounding on ahead and then coming back to us. Interestingly, he never took his eyes off his owner for more than a second. He constantly turned around to see whether we were following, changing direction or calling him back. And when larger dogs arrived threateningly on the scene, the dog knew where to look for support: to his owner, who was much bigger and more powerful than he was. This psalm, says Alec Motyer, teaches that, when troubles come, 'all that is needed is the "upward glancing of an eye", for our upward look meets the downward gaze of the One "whose throne is in heaven"'. When troubles come, keep your eyes looking up and wait patiently for the answer to come down.

ORIENTATION: Sublime simplicity is here combined with graphic imagery. It could apply to so many periods of her history, but probably relates to Philistine opposition to the young kingdom of Israel. Note the twice-repeated 'If the Lord had not been on our side . . .'

MAP: The psalm begins and ends with God.

The Lord who is for us, 1–2

The forces that were against us, 2–7

Israel has a feeling of being engulfed by trouble and overwhelmed, as if caught:

- in an earthquake, 3a;
- in a fire, 3a: 'anger flared';
- in a flood, 4–5;
- in the jaws of a wild beast, 6;
- in a trap, 7.

The God who is above us, 6–8

He is a God who:

- rescues his people, 6–7a;
- repels their enemies, 7b;
- renews his creation, 8.

LINK: Rom. 8:31–39 is the NT counterpart to this psalm in its consideration of what the phrase 'If God is for us . . .' means.

SIGNPOST: One of the interesting things about this psalm is its ordinariness. It may not seem ordinary to you and me to suffer from earthquakes, flash floods, wild-beast attacks and animal traps, though we may have a little experience of some of these, but it was the stuff of life in ancient Israel. Living close to raw nature made life precarious. Many psalms expressed confidence in God's deliverance from human enemies, but this one expresses confidence in God's help when faced by the natural antagonisms and frustrations of our world. God is not only 'on our side' when we face spiritual temptation or attack, but equally when the car breaks down, the washing machine leaks, the computer freezes, the motorway is blocked and the roof caves in! In these situations the remedy is just the same as when we're in the thick of spiritual warfare on some evangelistic campaign or mission trip. *Pray*. God is on our side in the ordinary frustrations of living!

Psalm 125

ORIENTATION: The title chosen for this psalm comes from Eugene Peterson's *A Long Obedience in the Same Direction*, in which he comments on 'the saw-toothed history of Israel' because there are so many ups and downs in it. Here the 'up' of confident faith lies right next to the 'down' of complete realism. Yet, whatever happens, they are always secure as God's people, surrounded by his loving protection.

 MAP: Here is:

A security to be enjoyed, 1–2
- as secure as the mountains around Jerusalem;
- so secure is God's love for them.

A reality to be confronted, 3
The above is all very well, but what about the ever-present reality of wickedness? It is real but limited, so the godly are not themselves forced to do evil.

A finality to be awaited, 4–5
Judgment of the wicked and vindication of the righteous will come and it is right to pray for it, but then patiently wait for it.

SIGNPOST: We had just finished viewing a house we might have bought when the owner said, 'I must show you this before you leave,' and introduced us to the CCTV system that provided the house with security. Curious, we thought, unless it's just that they like gadgets – until, that is, we found that it was located right next to a young offenders' facility! Security is big business these days. Just try having a phone conversation with your bank and you'll get nowhere until you've answered a mountain of security questions. National security, homeland security, house security, personal security, security cameras, security codes, security gates, security guards, security systems . . . it's everywhere. The need for security seems to lie deep within the make-up of most people. And God knows that, so he gives Israel, and us, the most wonderful assurance that they are secure. He personally surrounds and protects them as the mountains surrounded and protected Jerusalem. You can't get a better security guard than the King of the Universe. So why be afraid?

The Psalms and the Messiah

Jesus said to the disciples, 'This is what I told you while I was still with you: Everything must be fulfilled that is written about me in the Law of Moses, the Prophets and the Psalms' (Luke 24:44).

The Psalms were widely believed to promise the coming of a Messiah. People differ over the number of 'messianic psalms', and whether their authors originally understood themselves to be writing about the coming of a Messiah, but Christian scholars would all accept that there is at least a solid core of such psalms.

Messiah means 'anointed one' and it was the kings of Israel who were originally the anointed ones, with Samuel anointing both Saul and David in sequence (see 1 Sam. 9 and 16). Some psalms focus on this theme and extol both the character and the success of the king's reign. Psalms 2, 45, 72 and 110 are most notable in this connection. But these psalms claim rather too much if they apply merely to a human king. They may be expressions of hope and prayer, but none of the OT kings match up to the portrait painted. Moreover, it eventually became evident that the high hopes people had of David's family seemed to have been misplaced. As David's dynasty came to an end, so they came to believe that these psalms pointed to the coming of a future Messiah whose rule would measure up to expectations.

Christians naturally came to read psalms such as 16, 40, 68 and 118, as well as the royal psalms, not only as describing the Messiah but as fitting exactly the life of Jesus of Nazareth. The Gospel writers use the Psalms to explain what was happening with Jesus. For example, 2:7 is quoted in their accounts of the transfiguration and John cites 69:1 and 34:20 in his account of the crucifixion. Jesus also identifies himself with them when he especially makes Psalms 22 and 110 his own.

The Psalms prove to be a wonderful and detailed signpost pointing to Jesus the Messiah.

Psalm 126 ✓

 ORIENTATION: Like the other 'songs of ascent', this one reflects on the great things God has done. It looks as if the opening verses express joy at the return of the people from exile in Babylon. But it is realistic enough to admit that their restoration has not solved all the problems and that immense difficulties lie ahead of the small group of initial returnees. Ezra, Nehemiah and Haggai all speak of the challenges they faced. Hence God's continuing help in restoring their fortunes is still needed.

MAP: Thanksgiving for the past is mingled with tears for the present.

Past restoration is celebrated, 1–3
Especially its impact:
- in bringing joy to God's people, 1–2a;
- in bringing testimony to other nations, 2b–3.

Present restoration is sought, 4–6
The request for continued restoration is accompanied by several images:
- they seek a reversal of their fortunes, 4a;
- they seek refreshment in the desert, 4b;
- they seek rewards at the harvest, 5–6.

LINKS: This psalm echoes Psalm 85.

SIGNPOST: 'It will be different when . . .' How often people say that and how much more often do they think it. 'When we move, when we graduate, when we marry, when I get promotion . . . then life will be easier, pressures will be reduced, temptations will disappear . . .' Like Israel, 'we dream' and when we do so, the appropriate response is sometimes the popular one: 'Dream on.' Changing our circumstances is often not the answer to our problems, not least because we go into the new situation taking our characters and weaknesses with us. Monks used to flee to the desert to avoid the temptations of Rome, only to find that they could take themselves out of Rome, but they could not take Rome out of themselves. When Israel arrived home after exile, it wasn't as easy as they had dreamed. Much rebuilding was needed, food was scarce, land quality was poor, divisions broke out among them and enemies still opposed them. So, even after the 'restoration', they needed God to 'restore' them. God's work of restoration in our lives is a daily need and a lifelong challenge.

We dreamed

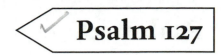

Psalm 127

ORIENTATION: Perhaps this psalm, like its predecessor, is set in the time after the exile when God's people were much occupied by rebuilding their homes and especially building a new home for God, the new temple (see Hag. 1:1 – 2:9). Some, however, say that it belongs to an earlier period and refers to the building of Solomon's temple.

MAP: There are two very distinct halves to this psalm and the relationship between them is not altogether clear, but there is a play on words in the Hebrew between 'builders' and 'sons'.

House building, 1–2
House building involves:
- the necessity of the Lord's help;
- the futility of unaided effort.

Home making, 3–5
The thought moves from the house as a building to the family who occupy it as a home:
- children are a divine blessing, 3;
- children are a natural expectation, 4;
- children are a wonderful support, 5.

SIGNPOST: Reliant Robin cars aren't seen much these days. Tiny three-wheelers, they always seemed a little unstable and would be quite vulnerable in today's traffic. I remember reading of one oversized owner who had taken to driving around with a sack of potatoes on his passenger seat. It was to give him balance, otherwise the car tipped on its side as soon as he got in! This is a balancing psalm that will not be greatly loved by those who suffer from a severe dose of the Protestant Work Ethic. Hard work, long hours, conscientious commitment and short-term investment for long-term gain are all commended in Proverbs as the way to success. And so they are. But this psalm gives the other side of the equation. All that is worthless 'unless the Lord builds the house'. And if he's the builder, then there's no need for drivenness. We can rest in him to produce the results. If he isn't the builder, the hard work will be futile and the drivenness likely to lead to a heart attack. Rejoice in the gift of sleep as a symptom not of indolence, but of trust in God.

Unless the Lord

Psalm 128

 ORIENTATION: The theme of 'labour' continues from the previous psalm, but this time from a different perspective. It is marked by a combination of unashamed revelling in and wise reflection on the blessing of God.

MAP: The blessing of God branches in three directions:

The blessing of God: a prerequisite, 1
This defines who may expect to be blessed by God. It is not for all, but for those who fear him. The second line, which speaks of obedience to God, is a way of explaining what it means to fear him.

The blessing of God: a promise, 2–4
Those who fit with v. 1 may legitimately expect God to bless them in at least two areas:
- fruitfulness in their work, 2;
- fruitfulness in their family, 3.

The blessing of God: a prayer, 5–6
The promise is now turned into prayer, the statement into a petition. It is evident that the blessing of God is not to be automatically assumed.

SIGNPOST: Our hostess was somewhat apologetic and embarrassed as we sat down to a sumptuous Sunday lunch. The problem was certainly not a shortage of anything. The problem was that the guest of honour was George Hoffman, the first full-time director of Tearfund. How could you not be embarrassed about the quantities (and quality!) of food available when you had a representative and advocate of the world's starving millions to dinner? George graciously set the hostess at ease with the perfect answer. 'Please don't apologize,' he said, 'for enjoying the prosperity that God intended all of us to enjoy. Don't feel guilty about what God intended to be normal for all. It is the poor who are not receiving what God planned.' Psalm 128 enables us to thank God without guilt for the rewards of our labours, when we see them not as a right, but as a result of his blessing. Neh. 8:10 wisely advises, 'Go and enjoy choice food and sweet drinks, and send some to those who have nothing prepared . . . Do not grieve, for the joy of the Lord is your strength.'

ORIENTATION: No-one knows who wrote this psalm, or when. But Israel's story is personified in the first part, which comes alive if read in the light of Nehemiah's experience of opposition when he was seeking to rebuild the wall of Jerusalem. See Neh. 4 and 6.

MAP: Two halves relate uneasily here.

Thanksgiving for survival, 1–4
Israel reflects on past experience, which is marked by:
- the persecution 'he' suffered, 1, 3;
- the perseverance 'he' demonstrated, 2;
- the preservation 'he' experienced, 4, from God.

Prayer for retaliation, 5–8
The focus is no longer personal, but on Zion and all that it stands for. Those who stand in opposition to Jerusalem are in reality expressing their hatred of the God of Jerusalem. For such the psalmist prays that:
- their progress will be blocked, 5;
- their lives will be short, 6–7;
- their ruin will be evident, 8.

LINKS: The cry for vengeance in vv. 5–8 groups this psalm with 35, 55, 69 and 109. Read their *Signposts* and the note on 'Psalms of vengeance' (p. 119).

SIGNPOST: We live in a victim culture – so much so that, according to Jonathan Sacks, who as Chief Rabbi is no stranger to the suffering of the Jews, we now engage in 'competitive victimhood' and seek to outdo each other in claiming victim status. In *The Home We Build Together* (Continuum, 2007) he writes, 'The psychology of victimhood is bad psychology. A victim is by definition an object not a subject, passive rather than active, a done-to rather than a doer. If you see yourself as a victim, then you locate the cause of your condition in something *outside* yourself. That means that you cannot change your situation. This is the condition Martin Seligman calls "learned helplessness", and it leads to depression, fear and resentment.' Psalm 129 suggests that Israel had every reason to consider themselves victims, but refused to accept that status. Their solution, however, was precisely to turn to the greatest *outside* help of all, their faithful God, rather than rely on a self-help programme.

Persecution and perseverance

Psalm 130 ✓

 ORIENTATION: On some days the light seems so pure that your vision is sharply focused and the colours vivid. That is the impression given by this psalm, which begins in deep despair and ends with 'plenteous grace' (Miles Coverdale's translation of v. 7). It is a psalm of confession that gives voice to an individual's lament.

MAP: The psalm moves through four stages.

Crying to God, 1, 2
From the depths, for mercy.

Forgiveness from God, 3–4
- The problem revealed, 3: the problem here is guilt, not trouble as elsewhere.
- The promise believed, 4: 'you offer forgiveness' (NLT).
- The purpose expressed, 5: so we reverently serve God.

Waiting for God, 5–6
- The psalmist doesn't rush to assume forgiveness glibly.
- Yet the psalmist keeps alert and eagerly seeks it.

Hoping in God, 7–8
With God is 'full redemption', 'unfailing love', redemption 'from all . . . sins'.

LINKS: Other confession psalms are found at 6, 32, 38, 51, 102 and 143.

SIGNPOST: The story of John Wesley's conversion on 24 May 1738 is well known. He later wrote in his *Journal* about that evening at Aldersgate Street, London: 'About a quarter before nine, while he [Martin Luther: his commentary on Romans was being read] was describing the change which God works in the heart through faith in Christ, I felt my heart strangely warmed. I felt I did trust in Christ, Christ alone for salvation; and an assurance was given me that He had taken away my sins, even mine, and saved me from the law of sin and death.' What is not so well known is that on the same afternoon Wesley had attended evensong at St Paul's Cathedral, where the anthem sung was Psalm 130. Wesley had been crying from the depths, searching for the assurance of salvation for some considerable time, and now had found it. The singing of this psalm with its great note of 'full redemption' prepared the way for his finding assurance that evening. Do we have a similar assurance that, whatever we may be guilty of, we are utterly forgiven?

The Psalms
and the life of Jesus

Growing up in the synagogue, Jesus would have heard the Psalms read or sung on a regular basis. The doxologies at the end of each book were routinely used to pronounce blessing on the worshippers, while the whole book was read either every year or over a three-year cycle. His family's annual pilgrimage to Jerusalem for the Passover, recorded in Luke 2:41, would have seen him singing the 'songs of ascents' with the rest of the travellers and exposed him to the awesome singing of the temple. The Psalms would have been ingrained in his thinking, and in the thinking of his disciples, and it is therefore not surprising that they are often alluded to in his ministry.

Leaving aside the period of his betrayal, passion and death, Jesus quotes several psalms in a way that daringly draws attention to his unique role. In Matt. 13:35 he explains his speaking in parables by reference to Psalm 78:2, while 118:22–23 is called into play with the image of the rejected stone which became the cornerstone. Jesus also takes v. 26 of the same psalm, 'Blessed is he who comes in the name of the Lord', to refer to himself (Matt. 23:39; Luke 13:35). The synoptic Gospels all quote Jesus citing the riddle of 110:1 concerning David's son also being his Lord. And he uses 8:2 to justify the praise of the children as he enters Jerusalem. In an argument with the Jews (John 10:34) Jesus quotes 82:6, and he cites 35:9 and 69:4 while speaking to his disciples in the Upper Room.

Others also use the Psalms as a vehicle to interpret what was happening in Jesus. The heavenly voice from 2:7 is heard at Jesus' baptism and transfiguration. The disciples remember 69:9 as he cleanses the temple (John 2:17). The crowds both look for a sign, using 78:24–25 as a goad in John 6:31, and later welcome Jesus with the words of 118:26, according to Mark 11:9. And, knowing the influence of the Psalms on Jesus' life, even the devil tries to tempt him with a quotation from 91:11–12.

The Psalms shaped the consciousness of people in Jesus' day and by them they came to understand that God was at work in a unique way in him.

Psalm 131 ✓

Contentment *(vertical, left margin)*

 ORIENTATION: This psalm of David cannot be placed in any particular part of David's life. Charles Spurgeon said that it was 'one of the shortest Psalms to read, but one of the longest to learn'.

MAP: It commends the quest for:

Humility in character, 1a
We are schooled to sell ourselves. Humility is a virtue that is hard to gain and harder still to maintain.

Wisdom in perspective, 1b
Spurgeon again: 'We do well to know our own size,' and not to be concerned about matters that give us an inflated sense of self-importance.

Stillness in God, 2–3
Like the weaned child at rest in the mother's arms, we should be content because we are secure and trusting, and not striving. The bottom line of the psalm invites others to trust 'now and for evermore'.

LINKS: Key NT texts on contentment are Phil. 4:11–12; 1 Tim. 6:8; Heb. 13:5.

SIGNPOST: The psychologist Oliver James is among the many who have asked why Britain is more prosperous than ever before but less happy, especially as measured by the growing number of people who struggle with depression. His answer in *Britain on the Couch* (Century, 1997) is that we are a nation of 'wannabes'. As soon as we achieve one goal, the goalposts move, so we are permanently dissatisfied. More recently he has diagnosed that we are suffering from *Affluenza* (Vermillion, 2007), a contagious virus of envy that causes depression. Others in the growing field of research into happiness and well-being agree. Psalm 131 is profoundly counter-cultural in a pushy, get-ahead, improve-yourself society. It breathes the air of a contentment that our restless, never-satisfied society finds elusive. Spurgeon's comment, 'We do well to know our own size' is wise. Living wisely involves learning to be content with where God has put us and what God has made us, and would spare us a lot of destructive *angst*.

ORIENTATION: David's self-denying determination to ensure a dwelling place for the ark of the covenant (v. 8) is impressive. The background to the psalm is found in 2 Sam. 6 – 7. While this is about David, his throne and his Lord, it is more widely applicable to us because it concerns the nature of entering into a covenant with God.

MAP: The oath David swore to God (v. 2) is perfectly balanced by the oath God swore to David (v. 11).

David's oath to God, 1–10
His oath was to bring the ark to Jerusalem and find 'a place for the Lord'. Note:
- David's request, 1;
- David's commitment, 2–5;
- David's achievement, 6–10: this pictures the crowds gathering from all over Israel to celebrate the return of the ark to Jerusalem as told in 2 Sam. 6.

God's oath to David, 11–18
These verses speak of:
- the covenant God entered, 11–12;
- the choice God made, 13–14;
- the comfort God promised, 15–18.

SIGNPOST: It seems a lot of fuss to make about a box, even if it's a sacred object covered in gold and guarded by cherubim. But it's not the box that matters so much as what the box symbolizes. The ark was God's throne on earth and symbolized his presence among his people. David's enthusiasm to bring it to Jerusalem was in fact an enthusiasm for God to live among his people again. From one viewpoint, that sums up the Bible's message. God originally walked in Eden and conversed with Adam and Eve until sin caused them to hide from him. In the wilderness God lived in the tabernacle at the centre of Israel's camp, although the annual Day of Atonement (Lev. 16) was needed to remove sin's defilement from it. Now David wants God to live centrally again. The end of our salvation is the same. Although Jesus is present now among his people (Matt. 18:20) and within believers (Col. 1:27), we still look forward to the day when God lives among his people. Read Rev. 21 – 22 again and be inspired by the vision of which David has only a faint inkling.

The swearing of oaths

ORIENTATION: Again, as with Psalm 125, our title comes from Eugene Peterson's *A Long Obedience*. He interprets this psalm as a vision of a perfect community, the full reality of which will be experienced only in heaven.

MAP: There are three aspects here:

An observation, 1

Unity in the community is good. Conversely, by implication, disunity is to be avoided and proves costly, draining all concerned.

An illustration, 2–3, or rather two!

Unity functions like:

- Aaron's oil that symbolizes service. The background to this is found in the ordination rituals of Exod. 29, which record Aaron's initiation into the priesthood.
- Hermon's dew that symbolizes refreshment. The moisture of the morning is very welcome in contrast to the barren desert land of Israel.

An explanation, 3b

It is not merely that unity is an obviously good thing in itself; it is also that this is where God has chosen to distribute his blessing. The beneficial effects of unity do not just happen. They are actively caused by God.

SIGNPOST: You can get the best out of some works of art only by looking at them from different angles. The same is true of some scriptures, and this is one of them. The most straightforward angle is that of teaching. It is a wisdom psalm instructing us that if we want God's blessing we should live in harmony with our fellow believers, difficult though that may sometimes be! From another angle it is a testimony. The nation was never more united than it was under David and Solomon. David had fought hard over many years to secure its unity (2 Sam. 5:1–5) and when it was achieved they knew God's blessing. But, from yet another angle, it is also a warning. The nation's unity was fragile and easily broken. Sadly, after Solomon's death it broke in two and both parts began their long slide into corruption, warfare and exile. Unity matters to God. Disunity in his family grieves him. So we need to 'make every effort to keep the unity of the Spirit through the bond of peace' (Eph. 4:3). That's where the blessing is.

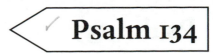

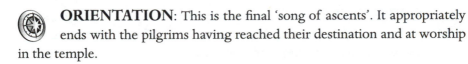 **ORIENTATION**: This is the final 'song of ascents'. It appropriately ends with the pilgrims having reached their destination and at worship in the temple.

MAP: This slender psalm seems almost too brief for comment, but three words about worship, variously translated into English, stand out.

Blessing, 1, 3
The TNIV begins with the word 'Praise'. Others use 'Bless'. God is both the object and the subject of blessing. Verse 1 encourages us to bless him, to offer him praise. In v. 3 he becomes the source of blessing, pouring grace and goodness into our lives. So there is a circle of blessing.

Service, 1b
The word 'minister' (TNIV) is a somewhat pious word. NLT uses the more down-to-earth 'serve' – it's what 'servants' (v. 1a) do. Worship is about praising and actions; about singing and doing. The Levites sang and prayed while serving as nightwatchmen, but they also had tasks to do during the long, unsociable hours of darkness. They acted as security guards, kept the fire going and the lamps burning, cleared up from the previous day's sacrifices and prepared things for the morning. It wasn't glamorous, but it was important service for the Lord.

Holiness, 2
Verse 2 literally says, 'Lift up your hands in holiness,' which most take to refer to the holy place, so it is often translated 'sanctuary'. It reminds us that obedience and right attitudes are required if blessing is to come to God's servants.

SIGNPOST: We arrived at church one holiday to be greeted by the vicar asking, 'Are you ordained?' It was a peculiar welcome! He explained that he was losing his voice and needed someone to take the Communion service. I gladly obliged. But 1 Pet. 2:9 and Rev. 1:6 tell us that all believers are priests. Churches have leaders and pastors, but there is no longer a special class of priests, like those who served in the temple. Every Christian has access to God through Jesus, the great priest, alone (Heb. 10:19–22). And every Christian is called to serve, some by leading worship and some by undertaking the more practical jobs, just like the priests and Levites of old. So, 'Are you ordained?'

The nightwatchmen

Psalm 135 ✓ >

 ORIENTATION: Psalms 135 and 136 link back to the *Hallel* psalms 111 – 118 with their command to praise the Lord. They may be an example of a hymn sung by pilgrims during the festivals.

MAP: Psalm 135 is a praise sandwich (vv. 1–2, 19–21) where the meat in the middle consists of recalling the big picture of Israel's experience of God. The central section recalls:

The Lord's goodness, 3–4

He is nothing but good, gracious and generous to Israel, whom he has chosen.

The Lord's greatness, 5–7

His ability to do whatever he pleases is illustrated by reference to the creation and the weather. In all of space, there are no limits or exceptions to his powers.

The Lord's salvation, 8–12

His salvation was irrefutably demonstrated in his defeat of Israel's enemies and his provision of land for them.

The Lord's renown, 13–14

His fame will be further enhanced by the way he will vindicate his people in the future.

The Lord's opponents, 15–18

While idols are impotent, the living Lord reigns all-powerful.

SIGNPOST: 'For the Lord is good' (v. 3). What a simple yet profound statement! God's character is summed up in this uncomplicated word 'good'. My dictionary gives almost forty different usages of the word. It is a pleasing virtue, an admirable and positive quality that speaks of moral excellence and proves beneficial to those who encounter it. It suggests kindness, generosity, genuineness and reliability. It is satisfying and sufficient. It is not marred or debased in any way. When the psalmists made this repeated claim they were not setting out a theoretical position, but speaking from personal experience. Psalm 13:6 says of Lord, 'for he has been good *to me*'. Psalm 84:11 affirms that he does not withhold good from those who follow him. Psalm 119:68 claims that he both *is* and *does* good. So the invitation comes, '*Taste and see* that the Lord is good' (34:8). How do we do that? According to that same verse, we do so by taking refuge in him. Can you say from personal conviction, 'Surely God is good . . . ' (73:1)?

The Psalms and
the cross of Jesus

The Psalms surface even more during the week of Jesus' passion than they did during his life. They are found on the lips of Jesus himself and in the words of the Gospel writers. They cover the whole time from his betrayal to his last breath.

Jesus quotes 41:9, 'Even my close friend, someone I trusted, one who shared my bread, has lifted up his heel against me', as Judas was about to betray him. John 13:18 gives us the full version, while the other Gospels allude to it. John may also be hinting at 55:12–15 in his quotation.

Best known is the cry of desolation (Matt. 27:46; Mark 15:34) that Jesus shouts as he hangs on the cross. 'My God, my God, why have you forsaken me?' is the first line of Psalm 22. The psalm ends on a positive note and opinion is divided as to whether, by quoting this first line, Jesus was intending to draw attention to the whole psalm and send a signal that deliverance would come, or not. Either way, the bleakness of his desertion should not be blunted.

Three times John speaks of the crucifixion as fulfilling the scriptures and each time he mentions a psalm. In John 19:23–24 he refers to the seamless robe of 22:18. In 19:28–30 John's reference is to 69:21 (also 22:15), where the victim's thirst is quenched. And in 19:36 John quotes 34:20: 'Not one of his bones will be broken.' This reminds us not only of the Psalms, but of the Passover lamb (Exod. 12:46), indicating how John understood the significance of Jesus' death.

Luke also quotes the Psalms in his crucifixion account. Luke 23:46 tells us that Jesus' final cry from the cross came from 31:5. It was a cry of trust and submission: 'Father, into your hands I commit my spirit.'

The death of Jesus caused people to reach deep into the spiritual psyche of Israel as expressed in the Psalms, and they found there a way of understanding what was happening at Golgotha.

Psalm 136 ✓

ORIENTATION: Reading the response 'His love endures for ever' twenty-six times, as this psalm requires us to do, may seem tedious – but imagine it sung antiphonally by a superb choir during one of Israel's great festivals. This is the last of the *Hillel* psalms that started at Psalm 120.

MAP: Observe the movement in the psalm from the magnificent opening summons (vv. 1–4), through Israel's specific experience (vv. 5–22), to its high claims at the end (vv. 23–26). We are called to give thanks because God is:

The supreme God, 1–4

The Creator God, 5–9

The saving God, 10–15

The protecting God, 16

The conquering God, 17–22

The merciful God, 23–24

The generous God, 25

The highly exalted God, 26

SIGNPOST: Within a marriage it is important for the partners to say 'I love you' at least once a day. It is dangerous to take the love for granted, for we soon ignore altogether what we take for granted. It's also important not to rely on actions and unspoken signals alone, significant though they are. We human beings were made to communicate with words. They help us express ourselves, our feelings, experiences and beliefs. But they also help us shape our understanding of things. No-one in Britain sees snow as the Inuit do, because we don't have the words for it. They have over twenty words for snow and perceive it altogether differently as a result. Words also make things more real. It isn't until we put things into words that we really grasp them. Experience is somehow incomplete unless we verbalize it. Our thinking, learning, seeing and feelings are confirmed as we articulate them. Words are powerful. They possess creative energy. They are anything but flat, 'mere words'. They rebound on us. So while it may seem tediously repetitious to keep saying, 'His love endures for ever,' it is important to do so, just as it is important to tell your partner that you love them. Taking God's love for granted means we are soon likely to forget it altogether. So let's say, 'His love endures for ever.'

 ORIENTATION: This poignant and beautiful lament was composed in exile or very shortly afterwards.

 MAP: The psalm revolves around the theme of memory.

'When we remembered': Memories can paralyse, 1–4

Remembering what used to be and how Jerusalem had been destroyed and its people captured reduced them to tears and silence, rather than leading them to song.

'If I forget': Memories may revitalize, 5–6

If remembering is sometimes very painful, forgetting is more dangerous! Keeping alive the memory of what Jerusalem once was moved them beyond despair and provided them with hope for the future and strength to persevere in the present.

'Remember, Lord': Memories will galvanize, 7–9

In the final section, the psalm shifts its focus from human memories to God's memory. His people pray that his memory will provoke him into action and that he would repay the Edomites (see Obadiah for an explanation) and the city of Babylon.

SIGNPOST: Charles Dickens's *A Tale of Two Cities* was a story about London and Paris at the time of the French Revolution. Much of the Bible, as in this psalm, is also a tale of two cities: Babylon and Jerusalem (Zion). From the exile on, Babylon became a symbol of captivity and oppression, much as Egypt was before her rise to power. The climax of Babylon's career in persecution and its final downfall is found in Revelation, where it serves as a code word for the city of Rome, then the current world power. Rev. 18 – 19 both laments and rejoices over Babylon's demise and uses it as a warning to other cities not to abuse their power. In contrast, Jerusalem is used as a symbol of peace (*shalom* is part of her name!) and well-being because God lives in her. So the actual city gives way to 'the new Jerusalem' in Rev. 21:2 where God will permanently dwell in safety with his people. What world city does Babylon represent today? In which city does your citizenship belong?

Psalm 138 ✓

 ORIENTATION: The final selection of David's compositions begins here and continues until Psalm 145. It is a very personal song that draws attention to three dimensions of praise.

MAP: This map is of the contours of praise.

Depth, 1–3

The very personal beginning of this psalm displays:
- a depth of emotion, 1;
- a depth of devotion, 2a: 'bow down';
- a depth of satisfaction, 2b–3: God honours his promises and answers our prayers.

Breadth, 4–5

From the personal to the universal: the psalm prays that kings across the wide earth will grasp the wisdom of the Lord and so see his glory and offer him worship.

Length, 6–8

David now reflects on the future and prays that the love of the exalted Lord (the height dimension is mentioned in passing in v. 6) might continue with him, the lowly one, to preserve his life in the future and, indeed, for ever!

SIGNPOST: Paul spoke of four dimensions to Christ's love in Eph. 3:17–19 when he prayed that the Ephesians would have power 'to grasp how wide and long and high and deep is the love of Christ, and to know this love that surpasses knowledge . . .' It may have been Paul's way of straining language to capture the totality and unity of God's love for us in Christ, but the different dimensions are worth considering even so. The width speaks of God's grace reaching all cultures, nations and ethnic groups (Rev. 5:11; 7:9). The length reminds us that his love is not a recent invention or afterthought, but springs from eternity (Eph. 1:4; Rev. 17:8). The height speaks of the exalted nature of his love that none can reach and overthrow (Rom. 8:31–39). It is secure. And the depth of his love is seen in the depth to which Christ stooped to secure our salvation (Phil. 2:5–11). Such is the extent of his love that, with David, we should bow down and praise his glorious name.

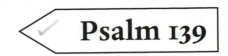

 ORIENTATION: We know nothing of the setting of this psalm, but it dwells on the most basic question of all: 'What is God like?'

 MAP: Four aspects of God's nature are revealed.

God's perception is wonderful, 1–6

His perception of:

- our inner thoughts, 1;
- our visible lives, 2–3, 5–6;
- our unspoken words, 4.

God's presence is unavoidable, 7–12

God's presence is:

- everywhere, 7–9;
- beneficial, 10;
- inescapable, 11–12.

God's power is amazing, 13–18

As seen in:

- the intricacies of an individual's creation, 13–16;
- the complexities of an individual's story, 16–18.

God's purity is humbling, 19–24

In its impact on:

- the wicked, 19–20;
- the righteous, 23–24.

SIGNPOST: I have heard some amazing testimonies about where people have found God. One was seeking to escape his Christian upbringing, so took a gap year in New Zealand. But God met him there and it was there he put his faith in Christ. Another spent a year in Israel, hardened against Christ all that time, but on the plane home he sat next to a Christian who led him to Christ, 35,000 feet up in the air! A third found Christ in a drug rehab centre, a fourth while in Paraguay. It truly is a question of 'Where can I go from your Spirit? Where can I flee from your presence?' (v. 7) This psalm speaks of God's *omnipresence* – that is, his presence everywhere throughout his creation. It also speaks of his *omniscience* – that his, his knowledge of everything (vv. 1–6), and of his *omnipotence* – that is, his power to accomplish anything he chooses (vv. 13–24). These are three great qualities of God that no other being shares. It's pointless trying to run from him. Why not rather rejoice that you are known so well by one who loves you (vv. 13–18)?

Psalm 140 ✓

 ORIENTATION: This psalm provides a further reflection on the conflict that marked so much of David's life. It gives some very sharp descriptions of his enemies. Though David's enemies could dominate the psalm, it is better to bring to the fore the positive claims made about God as David's personal God (v. 6).

MAP: The psalm looks in two directions simultaneously.

My enemies are:
- violent, 1;
- evil, 2;
- poisonous 3;
- arrogant, 5;
- mischief-making, 5;
- slanderous, 11.

But my God is:
- a safe keeper, 4;
- a Sovereign Lord, 7;
- a strong deliverer, 7;
- a source of justice, 12.

SIGNPOST: Powerful commercial interests in Birmingham were once seeking to redevelop an area in the city centre, but a little Quaker Meeting House stood in their way. They offered a generous amount to buy them out, but the Friends refused. The offer was raised, but still met with rejection. The developers were getting annoyed and began to send increasingly threatening letters, until they received a letter back from the small group that met in the Meeting House offering to buy them out! How could this be? Then the developers noticed that the letter was signed 'Cadbury'. The Cadbury family, of chocolate fame, who owned much of the city, belonged to that little Meeting House and would put their extensive wealth at its disposal. Things are not always what they seem. David's enemies may seem powerful, but David's God was even more so.

The Psalms
and the apostle Paul

Depending on how one counts them, there are about two dozen quotations from the Psalms in Paul's letters and a number of further allusions. They occur chiefly in Romans, and 1 and 2 Corinthians, with an isolated reference in Eph. 4:8 and a disputed one in Gal. 3:16.

Identifying the quotations is not as straightforward as it may seem, for several reasons. Paul did not use quotation marks, as we would do today, nor does he always say 'as it is written'. He sometimes quotes the Hebrew version and sometimes the Greek (Septuagint) translation of the OT and they do not always match exactly. On one occasion at least, in Eph. 4:8, he uses an interpretation of the text that reflects the way contemporary Jewish scholars would have handled it. So, instead of saying, 'When he ascended on high, he took many captives and *received* gifts from his people,' as Psalm 68:18 does, Paul says of Christ that he '*gave* gifts to his people'.

The psalms are mostly woven into his writings as descriptive justifications for the point Paul was making. In Romans he uses mostly negative verses to condemn humanity and advocate the justice of God (see Rom. 2:6; 3:4; 3:10–12; 11:9–10; 15:3). In a volley of quotations in Rom. 3:10–18, he runs snippets from six psalms together before concluding, in v. 20 that no-one is righteous before God, as 143:2 states. A glimmer of light interrupts this picture as the vision of the Gentiles praising the Lord crosses over from the Psalms (Rom. 15:9, 11) and as he rejoices in the blessing of sins forgiven (Rom. 4:7–8).

After a brief quote in 1 Cor. 3:20 denouncing the thinking of the wise as futile, Paul's main use of the Psalms in this letter is to affirm God's sovereignty (10:26; 15:25, 27). Two unconnected sayings from the Psalms occur in 2 Cor. 4:13 and 9:9.

Nothing hinges doctrinally on Paul's use of the Psalms. The impression given is rather that he was so steeped in them that he naturally resorted to using their words where appropriate as further confirmation of his argument.

A serious spirituality

 ORIENTATION: Derek Kidner entitles this psalm 'No Compromise', and says, 'There is a Puritan vigour and single-mindedness about this psalm.' Verses 5–7 are difficult to interpret, but the clear thread is a serious quest for a pure life in the midst of a 'Vanity Fair' world.

MAP: The psalm unfolds as follows:

David prays for a guarded mouth, 3

David asks for a protected heart, 4
Prov. 4:23: 'Above all else, guard your heart, for everything you do flows from it.'

David lays claim to a cool head, 5–7
David prefers correction to falling into wickedness. Verses 6–7 develop this thought by pointing out where failing to heed rebuke and David's wise words leads to difficulties. The heedless die 'a cruel death' and their bones are 'scattered without a decent burial' (VanGemeren).

David aims for attentive eyes, 8–10
His eyes need to be fixed on God rather than roaming in an undisciplined way. In this way he will avoid the traps others have set for him, while they fall into them themselves.

SIGNPOST: Travelling in David's day was a dangerous business. Added to the natural risks of getting lost, running out of water and being attacked by wild animals, there were also the ambushes deliberately set by various assailants and crooks. Evil people were out to cause his downfall and he needed God's providence to save him from falling foul of their schemes (see v. 8 and 35:1; 38:12; 140:5). The entrapments we face on our spiritual journey remain as serious as ever. Evil people who take no delight in our faith or our success are still at work. But if human agents of evil seem absent, there is an evil one prowling around 'like a roaring lion' (1 Pet. 5:8). That's why Jesus taught us to pray, 'Deliver us from the evil one' (Matt. 6:13). Many Christian leaders have fallen into the traps that have been laid because they thought themselves immune from danger and were not alert enough to it. Billy Graham has been a wonderful exception precisely because he has maintained vigilance. Be alert and pray (Matt. 26:41; Luke 21:36).

 ORIENTATION: Arising out of David's experience recorded in 1 Sam. 22 when he was, as it were, in 'the lion's den', this psalm is a cry for help by an individual who feels totally deserted. This is the final lament in the Psalms.

MAP: The cry is marked by:

Intensity, 1–2
'I cry aloud . . . lift up . . . pour out . . . '

Internalization, 3–4
The intense loneliness is internalized, giving rise to some classic symptoms of depression: a faint spirit and a feeling that no-one cares.

Intimacy, 5
From the depth of despair David begins to recover a little perspective and realizes that there is one who is committed to him and does look out for him – and that is the Lord, the God who has entered into a covenant with him. Without others to support him, the exclusive relationship between God and David becomes quite intimate. God is his refuge and his lot in life, and what is better than that?

Intention, 6–7
David pleads with God to listen to him and rescue him so that God's own name might be praised.

LINKS: The psalm is paralleled by Psalm 52.

SIGNPOST: It sounds full of self-pity and complaint. How can this psalm and similar laments be worthy prayers to bring to God? Walter Brueggemann explains that they are to be thought of as an 'act of faithfulness' because they are 'premised on the reliability and accessibility of God, on a vision of the way the world is supposed to be and is not . . . the lament characteristically expresses faith *sola gratia* (in grace alone). The speaker is aware that his destiny is in God's hand. The speaker is helpless and does not doubt that Yahweh can and may transform the situation'. So there's more than one way to complain! Your laments can be coloured by cynicism and mistrust, or by faith and hope. The Lord listens to those who through tearful cries throw themselves on him, trusting that his grace will be available.

Psalm 143 ✓ >

ORIENTATION: This is the last penitential psalm. David's situation is grave, but the psalm has a lighter tone than some. The thrust of his prayer is that God may lead him 'forward on a firm footing' (v. 10, NLT).

MAP: The psalm provides a good introduction to prayer.

The foundation of prayer, 1

The foundation of prayer is never our need, but always lies in the character of God, who is faithful, righteous and perfect.

The premise of prayer, 2

God's perfection is in contrast to human sin, which needs to be confessed as we approach God before petitions are made.

The substance of prayer, 3–10

His request for protection and guidance is summed up in v. 10: that he might be led 'on level ground' (TNIV). The fact that the path is slippery and likely to cause him to fall is due to:

- doubt, 2;
- danger, 3;
- depression, 4–7;
- deviation from the path.

The urgency of prayer, 6–7

David's tone is one of desperation. Our prayers are often not driven by the same sense of need, which is perhaps why we don't see too many answers.

The purpose of prayer, 11–12

As always, the purpose is God's glory: 'for your name's sake'.

SIGNPOST: A pastor friend in Vancouver, the other side of the world, rang very early one morning to ask me to visit one of his church members in our local hospital. The day before, Alan had been walking on our coastal path and lost his footing. He had to be rescued by air ambulance. Ironically, I had seen the news report on our local news the previous evening. Alan spent months recovering from serious spinal injuries until he was on his feet again and able to return home. Some paths are more slippery than others, but none of us plans to lose our footing. It happens suddenly. Spiritually we can lose our footing when disappointment comes, failure happens, pressures mount, when faith is challenged, or when we feel let down by God or others. It's worth praying often, 'May your Spirit lead me forward on a firm footing' (see v. 10).

 ORIENTATION: The commentators speak of this psalm as a mosaic and point out that it borrows phrases from Psalm 18.

MAP: The theme of divine strength and human weakness runs through it all.

Divine strength is described, 1–2

God is a rock, military trainer, fortress, stronghold, deliverer, shield and over-comer ('who subdues peoples under me'), but he is also 'my loving God'.

Human weakness is defined, 3–8

- it is inherent, 3–4: people are mere breaths;
- it is situational, 5–8: because of powerful enemies.

Divine strength is extolled, 9–10

David bursts into song in celebration of God's strength used on his behalf.

Human weakness is exposed, 11

Life is uncertain because of David's enemies, 11.

Divine blessings are celebrated, 12–15

The blessing of God enriches human life and ensures security in an unsafe world.

SIGNPOST: Visiting a folk museum on the Isle of Skye, I learned that it was within recent memory that electricity had reached the island. A journalist had asked one old crofter what difference it had made to him. 'Oh,' he replied, 'it's marvellous. When dusk falls I can turn on the electric light and that makes it so much easier to light my oil lamp.' Though he had the advantage of the brilliant light generated by electricity, he chose to live by the dim light of his old lamp. This psalm doesn't dwell in the spiritual half-light, but revels in the floodlights of God's blessing on human lives. Verse 3 should be read with a tone of puzzle and surprise. Why does God bother with us tiny human beings? Hasn't he got other things to do, like running the solar system? But he takes trouble with us and pride in us! David lists some of the evidence: God equips according to need (1), he protects (2), he cares (3), he rescues (7), he delivers (10), he prospers (12–14) and he safeguards (14). Blessing indeed. Israelite believers knew how to celebrate. When God prospered them, they 'revelled in [his] great goodness' (Neh. 9:25). Have we forgotten how to party?

Psalm 145 ✓ ⟩

 ORIENTATION: This magnificent psalm, the last psalm of David to be included, draws so much of the teaching and praise of the Psalms together in a superbly crafted acrostic poem. Its view of God is seen through a wide lens.

MAP: Consider it as if it were a great symphony.

The members of the orchestra, 1–10
- the solo artist whose melody is about God's greatness, 1–3;
- the dominant section ('generations') whose harmony is about God's works, 4–9;
- the whole orchestra ('all your works') whose theme is God's glory, 10–21.

The music of the orchestra, 1–21

- his works, 4;
- his power, 6;
- his righteousness, 7, 17;
- his faithfulness, 13;

- his majesty, 5;
- his goodness, 7, 9;
- his sovereignty, 11–13;
- his providence, 14–20.

The melodies of the orchestra, 14–20
- he restores the weary, 14;
- he feeds the hungry, 15–16;
- he meets the expectant, 18–19;
- he protects the believer, 20.

SIGNPOST: God spoke to me very personally through this psalm one morning. I was just about to go off to Bible college, but wasn't sure how my studies were to be financed. I had already received a grant to study at university and it was optional as to whether the local authority would support me further. I had just received a letter from them telling me they wouldn't give me a penny when I turned to this psalm in my routine readings. It was wonderfully reassuring. My eyes looked to the Lord and received the encouragement that he would provide for my needs generously (vv. 15, 16). And he did. I can say, 'The Lord is trustworthy' (v. 13). Go through the psalm and note the five sentences that begin, 'The Lord is . . . ' (vv. 3, 9, 13, 17, 18) and the other sentences where 'the Lord' is the subject (vv. 14, 15, 16, 19, 20). Is this the Lord to whom you say, 'Every day I will praise you and extol your name for ever and ever' (v. 2)?

The Psalms and the letter to the Hebrews

Given that it is steeped in an understanding of OT ways, it is not surprising that Hebrews contains numerous quotations from the Psalms, eighteen in all. They stretch from the first to the last chapter, from Heb. 1:5 to 13:4, and are taken from eleven psalms.

Several psalms are of particular importance to the writer. The royal psalms 2 and 110 are used, sometimes in tandem, to draw attention to the superiority of Jesus as both royal Son and Priest of the order of Melchizedek (Heb. 1:5, 13; 5:2, 6; 6:17, 21). Three other quotations from the psalms are found in Heb. 1 in support of Christ's superiority to angels, while in 2:6–8 Psalm 8 is brought into play in his argument that Christ is superior to other human beings.

Psalm 95's stern warning against testing God by not listening to his voice is made use of on four occasions in the warning sections of the letter (3:7–11, 15; 4:3, 7), especially vv. 7–8: 'Today, if you hear his voice, do not harden your hearts.'

In a very significant passage on the atonement, the writer makes an interesting use of the Greek version (LXX) of Psalm 40:6–8. He is drawing a strong contrast between the ultimately unsatisfactory nature of sacrifices under the old covenant and the completely satisfactory nature of the sacrifice of Christ under the new covenant. Instead of endless animal sacrifices, he argues on the basis of the psalm that the one thing God longed for was a person ('a body') who would live a life of perfect obedience ('as it is written about me . . . I have come to do your will, my God'), thus fulfilling the covenant's requirements without qualification. These words, the author says, referred to Christ. He alone has pleased God by his perfect active obedience to the law and his perfect passive submission to death. He is the sacrifice to end all sacrifices, as Psalm 40 foresaw.

Citations from Psalms 22 (Heb. 2:12) and 118 (Heb. 13:6) may seem more incidental, but demonstrate that the Psalms formed the warp and woof of the writer's mindset.

Psalm 146

 ORIENTATION: Contemporary culture is riddled with mistrust. We live in a surveillance society, have procedures to check compliance in every area, and doubt the words and promises of public figures. But there is one we can trust, as this, the first of five praise songs that conclude the Psalms, testifies.

MAP: After the introduction (vv. 1–2) the psalm falls into two halves.

Misplaced trust, 3–4

It is unwise to trust:

- whom?, 3: 'powerful people', NLT;
- why?, 4: because their transience makes their plans and promises precarious. Other reasons could also be given.

Well-placed trust, 6–10

It is wise to trust God because he is:

- the Creator, 6a, and so has power;
- the truthful one, 6b, and so keeps his promises;
- the righteous one, 7, 8c, and so always acts justly;
- the compassionate one, 7, 9, and so cares for the underdog;
- the Saviour, 8, and so moves beyond feeling to action;
- the holy one, 9, and so frustrates the plans of the wicked;
- the enduring one, 10, and so reigns for ever.

SIGNPOST: Our credit cards were stolen just before I was setting off for a visit to Australia and they couldn't be replaced in time. Travelling to the other side of the world for several weeks without a credit card to rely on and with no means of getting money out of an ATM was an interesting experience. It taught me just how much we rely on these little bits of plastic to get us through. What comfort and assurance they bring! Verse 3 says, 'Do not put your trust in princes, in human beings, who cannot save.' Psalm 118:9 offers similar advice. In our careers we stake our hopes on promises made, in our church we trust what leaders say, in our lives we trust the pledges made by others, only too often to be disappointed. People seldom intend to let us down, but, as this psalm warns, 'They're only human.' There is only one in whom we can place our trust without hesitation. How would you complete the sentence, 'I place my trust in . . . '?

CHIASTIC ~ ADJECT FROM CHIASM ....
Parallel in reverse order ~
'eat to live, not live to eat.'

✓ Psalm 147

How right it is to praise God

ORIENTATION: This community hymn of praise has to do with the challenges faced by the returning exiles (v. 2). It may originally have been three psalms put together. Verses 1–6 speak of God's plan for Jerusalem; 7–11 of his care for creation; and 12–18 of his rule from Zion.

MAP: In its present form, after the title verse, I find a fivefold chiastic structure helpful.

God's works, 2–6
Seen in:
- the redemption of the broken-hearted;
- the creation of the stars.

Sing to the Lord, 7–9
For the evidence of his power in creation.

God's ways, 10–11
God does not take pleasure in animal or human strength, but in people's holiness and faith.

Extol the Lord, 12–14
For the evidence of his providence in Jerusalem.

God's words, 15–20
His word is:
- effective in creation, 15–18;
- revealed to Jacob, 19–20.

LINKS: This psalm complements Job 37 – 39; Psalms 33 and 104; Isa. 40.

SIGNPOST: The Psalm skilfully weaves together some amazing pairings that are often thought to conflict with each other. It speaks of God's special care for Israel (vv. 2, 12–14, 20) and his genuine care of the whole earth (vv. 8–9). It balances his tenderness (v. 3) with his transcendence (v. 4). It highlights his power *and* his wisdom (v. 5), which are not always found together in human terms. Gordon Jackson translates this verse as 'Our God is amazing, his power is tremendous, and his wisdom is equal to every challenge.' It testifies that his works (vv. 2–6) and his words (v. 19) are one. Only at one point is the pairing fractured. He does not take pleasure in military strength (v. 10), to which the returning exiles might look, but in his people's trust and in their following his ways (v. 11). This God was exactly what people needed as they struggled to rebuild their community. It was 'fitting to praise him!'

Psalm 148

ORIENTATION: The summons to praise God here is broadcast through the widest possible networks. The command reaches to the highest parts of our universe (vv. 1–4), but, having embraced them, it narrows down at the end to 'the people close to his heart' (v. 14). It is amazing that once again people are seen as the summit and true centre of creation.

MAP: The psalm begins with the widest possible lens (vv. 1–6) and then replaces it with a narrower one (vv. 7–13) before ending with a close-up (v. 14).

Cosmic praise, 1–6

- The summons, 1–4: celestial bodies, both animate and inanimate, are called on to offer praise.

- The reason, 5–6, is that he created them and firmly established them.

Creation praise, 7–14

- The summons, 7–12: terrestrial bodies, both animate and inanimate, high and low, are summoned to offer praise.

- The reasons, 13–14, are twofold: first, his name is uniquely exalted, 13; second, his people are uniquely strengthened, 14.

SIGNPOST: The sheer audacity of this psalm is breathtaking. Tiny Israel calls on heaven and earth to praise her God as the one who 'alone is exalted'. Nature, the animal creation and the nations of the earth, with all their own and varied beliefs, are summoned alongside the planets and stars, indeed, the whole universe, to worship him. This psalm inspired the words of Francis of Assisi's hymn, 'All creatures of our God and king, lift up your voice and with us sing', and the opening lines of John Henry Newman's hymn, 'Praise to the holiest in the height, and in the depth be praise'. They are both worth singing as an aid to understanding this psalm, for in the end this is a psalm to be sung, not dissected! Even so, this is more than poetic licence. It makes a startling theological claim that there is one God and it does so on the grandest scale of all. That has huge implications for the world in which we live.

 ORIENTATION: The previous three psalms moved in ever-widening circles. The first was an individual's hymn, the second a community hymn and the third a cosmic hymn of praise. This psalm picks up some of their threads as it returns to offer more personal praise within the community.

MAP: Three features characterize the song Israel is invited to sing.

It is a fresh song, 1

It is to be newly composed to express joy for the victory recently won. It is not recycled material, but freshly written and sung.

It is a victory song, 2–5

God's gift of victory reminds them of their relationship to him. They are:

- creatures of a Maker, 2a;
- citizens of a king, 2b;
- recipients of a benefactor, 4a;
- celebrants of a victory, 4b;
- loyal subjects of a lord, 5a;
- dependents on a protector, 5b.

It is a battle song, 6–9

The song celebrates that:

- enemies, however powerful, are defeated;
- and justice, however severe, is delivered.

SIGNPOST: We're sometimes asked, 'What gives you pleasure?' Some find it in their family, some in sport, some in music, some in a box of chocolates! Running through the previous three psalms has been the thought of what gives God pleasure. And the answer is always the same: it is his people. Psalm 146:8 says, 'The Lord *loves* the righteous.' Psalm 147:11 says, 'The Lord *delights* in those who fear him.' Psalm 148:14 speaks of them as 'close to his heart'. Psalm 149:4 sums them all up with 'The Lord takes delight in his people'. I guess it is true that most fathers derive pleasure from watching their children grow and reach their potential. But it is somewhat daunting to think that God derives his pleasure from me. Not everything I do will please him. These psalms make it clear that I really delight him when I fear him and live a righteous life. Will I cause God grief or pleasure today?

Psalm 150 ✓

 ORIENTATION: Psalm 150 acts as a wonderfully brief but fitting conclusion to the whole book of Psalms.

 MAP: Basic questions are answered in this psalm.

What? 1

- Praise the Lord for his presence on earth.
- Praise the Lord for his reigning in heaven.

Why? 2

- Because of what he has done: 'his acts of power'.
- Because of who he is: 'surpassing greatness'.

How? 3–5

- Inclusively: the whole orchestra is invited to join in the music.
- Enthusiastically: they are encouraged to join in a wild celebration that holds nothing back.

Who? 6

Everything.

- Not just people, but all of creation.
- Not just the covenant people, but all the nations.

SIGNPOST: The brakes are off. The restraint is released. The conclusion to the book of Psalms is one of uninhibited praise, of self-abandoning joy. The journey to this point has had its low as well as its high points. The book has been nothing other than utterly realistic. There have been expressions of anguish in defeat, perplexity in darkness, despair in uncertainty, tears for suffering, sorrow at sin, crying for forgiveness, rage against injustice, fuming against evil, longing for direction and quiet reflections on life. There has equally been celebration of God as king, saviour, wisdom, lawgiver, shepherd, benefactor and protector. But, when all is said and done, we are left with simple, inclusive, universal praise for the God who was and is and is to come. The only appropriate response to the drama of our lives is doxology. 'Doxology', writes Walter Brueggemann, 'is an irrational act that pushes beyond control, summons us beyond our cherished rationality, rescues us from anxiety, transcends despair, overrides arrogance, strips us of self-sufficiency, and leaves us unreservedly and entirely entrusted to [God] who cares for us more than we care for ourselves.' It is our chief end 'to glorify God'.

A fitting crescendo

The Psalms and
the book of Revelation

With its five hundred or more references, Revelation refers more to the OT scriptures than any other NT book. The Psalms are the fourth most important source for John, after Isaiah, Ezekiel and Daniel respectively. Lengthy direct quotations may not be numerous, but many phrases and images from the Psalms seep quite naturally into his writing.

Both books concern the reign of God and so the resonance between them is hardly surprising. Revelation pictures a global rebellion where world powers rise up in opposition to God and persecute his people, and reveals God's plan for suppressing the rebellion through his Son with the result that he reigns unconquerable over all. Four aspects of the story draw us back to the Psalms.

First, there is the lament of the saints as they face persecution, which echoes the frequent bewilderment expressed in the Psalms as the righteous suffer. The cry 'How long, O Lord?' (Rev. 6:10) repeats the questions of Psalms 6:3; 13:1; 35:17 and many others.

Second, there is the good news that God will overthrow his enemies through his Son, whom he will install as King and who 'will rule with an iron sceptre'. This quotation from Psalm 2:9 is found three times in Revelation (2:27; 12:5; 19:15). With Revelation's wider use of Psalm 2, John clearly understood Jesus to be the Son of God (2:2) who would rule with justice universally.

Third, the victory songs that celebrate the downfall of Babylon (the symbol of opposition) in Rev. 18 – 19 mirror the psalms of vengeance in their quest for judgment to fall on their enemies. Rev. 18:6, for example, comes from 137:8.

Fourth, in its picture of the new Jerusalem (Rev. 21 – 22), Revelation draws on and exceeds the image of the old Jerusalem that was so celebrated in the Psalms.

Numerous other details, such as God being clothed in light, incense, lifting up holy hands, names written in the book of life, evoke the memory of the Psalms.

The Psalms and Revelation have one message: 'Great and marvellous are your deeds, Lord God Almighty. Just and true are your ways, King of the nations . . . For you alone are holy . . . ' (Rev. 15:3–4, from 86:9 and 111:2–3).

Afterword

The Psalms have taken us to the heights where we have had a clear sight of God's goodness and a vision of the grandeur of our salvation, where we joined in singing songs of joy. They have also taken us to the depths and assured us that we are not alone as we walk through the valleys of life, with all their shadows and fears. There, the Psalms helped us put into words the turmoil we often feel deep down. Sometimes they gave us ways to pray in ordinary days, when life seems routine and when nothing much, either good or bad, is happening. On such days they pointed to God's providence and his ordinary blessings, and encouraged us to be faithful to the one whose love is unfailing. On other occasions, they have pointed out pitfalls on the road ahead and prepared us to avoid the stumbling blocks of life. And when we have failed to do so, and fall into sin, they have given us a way to recover and get on the road again with God.

In these and other ways the Psalms have proved a true companion on the journey of faith. Since they are a true companion, we need to make them a constant companion. Reading them once, or even occasionally, will never enable us to plumb their depths or grasp their richness. We delight in the company of valued companions and, in like manner, it will prove immensely beneficial to our faith to spend much time with the Psalms.

Various strategies will help us to know them better. Read them regularly. Keep a notebook in which to write down 'a thought from each psalm'. Even try to write your own overview, capturing the main theme of each psalm.

Choosing a particular verse from a psalm to meditate on will surely prove helpful. Meditation is the art of chewing something over in a prayerful context. It's usually helpful to ask various questions of the verse, or passage – whom is it speaking about, what does it say, when does it apply? Or we might ask, is there here a lesson to learn, a promise to believe, a prayer to pray, an error to avoid, a perspective to adopt, a truth to accept? Meditation always leads us to turn our thoughts God-wards and to make truths a matter of the heart, rather than only of the mind.

Memorization is another way to benefit from the Psalms (and other parts of the Bible). It has become something of a lost art among Christians who have become confused by the number of Bible versions that exist and have reacted against rote learning and proof texting. But there is wonderful strength spiritually in being able to know God's word confidently and quote it unhesitatingly, even if you are saying it only to yourself! To do this, choose one version of the Bible and stick to it. You'll find the more poetic versions easier to remember than some of the more paraphrased ones. Note key verses that have spoken to you, write them out on a small card, carry them with you, and repeat them until you know them.

Then stand back and review at times. What are the main themes that are emerging? In particular, what picture of God and how he relates to his world arises from the Psalms? How do the Psalms point to the coming of Christ and our future destiny? Other themes such as suffering, doubt, families, unity, justice and creation, to name but a few, will also come to your mind.

Don't forget that the Psalms were the hymn book of Israel. They are meant to be sung, and sung in the company of others, rather than studied in isolation. How much easier it is to pick things up through song, rather than through the spoken word alone. We often find ourselves humming the tune and repeating the words of a song and then, before long, we find that the words have become ingrained in our minds. How much more profitable to let the words of the Psalms mould our attitude and perception, rather than those of a contemporary secular song.

One final suggestion. Why not as a church arrange a *PsalmFest*? In such an event, the Psalms could be presented through artwork, music, drama, testimony and guided meditation. Since the Psalms are so related to everyone's experience of life, and given that they already have a place in our wider culture, the *PsalmFest* need not be limited to members of the church. Local schools may be encouraged to contribute to the project and other members of the community may well have a part to play. It could serve as a great bridge to people who are not regular worshippers in church.

The Psalms provide us with a wonderful resource for the journey of faith. But they are of no use unless we make use of them. May you prove them to be 'a lamp to your feet and a light for your path' (119:105).

For reference and further reading

Brueggemann, Walter, *The Message of the Psalms*, Minneapolis: Augsburg, 1984.

———, *The Psalms and the Life of Faith*, ed. Patrick Miller, Minneapolis: Fortress, 1995.

Bullock, C. H., *Encountering the Book of Psalms*, Grand Rapids: Baker Academic, 2001.

Jackson, Gordon, *The Lincoln Psalter*, Manchester: Carcanet, 1997.

Kidner, Derek, *Psalms 1 – 72*, Tyndale Old Testament Commentaries, Leicester: IVP, 1973.

———, *Psalms 73 – 150*, Tyndale Old Testament Commentaries, Leicester: IVP, 1975.

Lewis, C. S., *Reflections on the Psalms*, London: Collins, 1961.

Motyer, Alec, *Treasures of the King: Psalms from the Life of David*, Nottingham: IVP, 2007.

Motyer, Alec, *Journey: Psalms for Pilgrim People*, Nottingham: IVP, 2009.

Peterson, Eugene H., *A Long Obedience in the Same Direction*, Downers Grove: IVP, 2nd ed. 2000.

Spurgeon, Charles, *Psalms*, Vols. I and II, The Crossway Classic Commentaries, Wheaton: Crossway Books, 1993.

VanGemeren, A., 'Psalms', in *The Expositor's Bible Commentary*, ed. Frank E. Gaebelein, Grand Rapids: Zondervan, 1991, 3–880.

Wilcock, Michael, *The Message of Psalms 1 – 72*, The Bible Speaks Today, Leicester: IVP, 2001.

———, *The Message of Psalms 73 – 150*, The Bible Speaks Today, Leicester: IVP, 2001.

Wright, Tom, *Simply Christian*, London: SPCK, 2006.

In addition, preachers may find the following commentaries helpful:

Grogan, Geoffrey, Two Horizons Commentary on the *Psalms*, Grand Rapids: Eerdmans, 2008. This came too late to be incorporated in the book, but will prove a rich, especially theological, resource to many. Probably the most helpful commentary for preachers.

Knight, G. A. F., *Psalms*, Vols. I and II, The Daily Study Bible, Edinburgh: St Andrew Press; Philadelphia: Westminster Press, 1982, 1983.

Mays, J. L., *Psalms*, Interpretation, Louisville: John Knox Press, 1994.

Wesier, A., *The Psalms*, Old Testament Library, London: SCM, 1962. An older commentary advancing a particular and now unpopular argument about a New Year covenant festival, which is nonetheless full of spiritual insight.